IMAGES
of America

LOS ANGELES
UNDERWORLD

Sgt. Russell Peterson inspects the murder weapon used to dispatch 42-year-old Mickey Cohen's bodyguard, Johnny Stompanato. Wielding the knife was Cheryl Crane, the 14-year-old daughter of Stompanato's girlfriend, famed actress Lana Turner. Turner and Stompanato's violent relationship came to a close on April 4, 1958. Hearing yet another fight and threats of physical abuse, young Cheryl grabbed a carving knife purchased earlier that day and reacted. But many believe it was Turner herself who killed the gangster and avoided prosecution by having her teenage daughter take the rap. (Niotta Collection.)

ON THE COVER: Jimmy Rist, Sol Davis, Mickey Cohen, and Mike Howard are booked on suspicion of murder in Los Angeles, following the underworld slaying of Cohen henchman Harry "Hooky" Rothman. "I'll know who done it in an hour after I'm out," Cohen quietly declared, "but I won't tell." The slaying would launch "the Battle of the Sunset Strip," a gang war fully covered in Chapter Nine. (*Los Angeles Times* Photographic Archives, uclalat_1429_b45_53221.)

IMAGES
of America

LOS ANGELES
UNDERWORLD

Avi Bash and J. Michael Niotta, PhD

ARCADIA
PUBLISHING

Copyright © 2021 by Avi Bash and J. Michael Niotta, PhD
ISBN 978-1-4671-0638-2

Published by Arcadia Publishing
Charleston, South Carolina

Printed in the United States of America

Library of Congress Control Number: 2020947165

For all general information, please contact Arcadia Publishing:
Telephone 843-853-2070
Fax 843-853-0044
E-mail sales@arcadiapublishing.com
For customer service and orders:
Toll-Free 1-888-313-2665

Visit us on the Internet at www.arcadiapublishing.com

*For the inkmen in Hollywood
and for anyone hungry for the truth*

CONTENTS

ACKNOWLEDGMENTS

The authors would like to thank our families, friends, and colleagues who supported us in this endeavor. Many thanks go to Victor DiGiorgio, Marnix Brendel (www.headsofthefamily.nl), Polly Dragna-Gainor, the Southward Car Museum (www.southwardcarmuseum.co.nz), and Jean-Marie Michalski with Belgium Lion Photography (www.BelgiumLionPhotography.com) for contributing images. We would also like to acknowledge the following: fellow authors, researchers, and contemporaries Richard N. Warner, Justin Cascio, Warren Hull, Scott Deitche, Christian Cipollini, John Binder, William "Hammy" Oldfield, Kenny "Kenji" Gallo, Luellen Smiley, Meyer Lansky II and Dani Porter-Lansky, Fabien Rossat, Arthur Nersesian, John Costello, Bret Juliano, and Larry Henry; the Library Special Collections, Charles E. Young Research Library, University of California, Los Angeles (UCLA); the Department of Justice (DOJ) for fulfilling Electronic Freedom of Information Act (eFOIA) requests for federal files, the Federal Bureau of Investigation (FBI) Vault, the Mary Ferrell Foundation, Ancestry, MyHeritage, and the California Digital Newspaper Collection (UCR); Marianna Gatto and the Italian American Museum of Los Angeles, Steve Lawson and David Finnern of California Wreck Divers and the Los Angeles Chapter of the Adventurers Club, Geoff Schumacher and the rest of the staff at the Las Vegas Mob & Law Enforcement Museum, members of the Los Angeles Mafia Facebook group, and lastly, Craig Timmins, Alan "Gunner" Lindbloom, Casey McBride, David Breakspear, Gary Jenkins, Nev Morgan, Rob Bailot Jr., and all the other fine chaps affiliated with the National Crime Syndicate website, where portions of this work previously appeared in Niotta's column "The Early Days of Los Angeles." To learn more about the authors, visit Avi Bash at www.bashcollection.com and Dr. J. Michael Niotta at www.jmichaelniotta.com.

INTRODUCTION

Over half a century before the rapid increase in street gangs earned Los Angeles the title of "Gang Capital of America," another type of crime and criminal filled the streets of Los Angeles; one that gave the same impression of glamour and appeal as the very movies produced in the Hollywood studios next door. While organized crime out west never achieved the same level of national notoriety as New York or Chicago, its cast of characters proved just as colorful and captivating as their more infamous contemporaries. And what came to pass certainly made for a fantastic picture. Even when crime on the streets resulted in murder, the black-and-white photographic coverage combined with the backdrop of the city somehow made these crime scenes almost as artistic as they were gruesome. A handful of earlier authors grasped this general idea.

Sunshine and Wealth, Bruce Henstell's visual storyteller from the mid-1980s, brought the lively and corrupt Los Angeles of the Roaring Twenties and 1930s to vivid life. Magically, somehow even the criminals captured in frame always seemed to wear a smile. At the close of the decade that followed, Jim Heimann—the art director on Henstell's project—returned to the theme, covering the darker, dustier, and seedier side of Los Angeles kept from the pages of the previous installment. Ushering in the forties and fifties, Heimann's *Sins of the City: The Real Los Angeles Noir* (1999) served as a perfect accompaniment, providing titillating stills of jumping clubs, hubbub cafés, and the gambling dens of the booming war years, plus the territorial spats among rival gangsters that erupted on the cusp of the 1950s. Just over a decade later, in 2011, Ernest Marquez snapshotted a much smaller segment of the City of Angel's unique history, encapsulating the era of the floating casinos that plied their wares defiantly offshore in the waters just outside Los Angeles and Orange County limits. Showcasing an extensive collection of gambling souvenirs, photographs, and paraphernalia, Marquez chronicled the early days of the water gamblers like no other. A few years earlier, Chris Nichols provided a comparable land-based offering, showcasing *The Leisure Architecture of Wayne McAllister* (2007). McAllister not only rubbed elbows with famed Los Angeles and Las Vegas gamblers—from Agua Caliente to the Biltmore Bowl to Clifton's Cafeteria, the Fremont, and the Desert Inn—he built their hangouts and gambling establishments.

Collectively, these works depict Los Angeles in magnificent splendor, and yet one vital story remains untold from each visual retelling. That is until now. Focusing much of the camera work on the birth, rise, and fall of the Los Angeles Brugad—or mafia family—*Los Angeles Underworld* carves out this little told and usually misrepresented niche. Through political plays and all-out warfare, this deadly and dreaded organization muscled into the lush rackets of the Spring Street gamblers that graced the pages of Henstell, Heimann, Nichols, and Marquez's work. Restaurateur turned politician Clifford Clinton dubbed this collective, which ran Los Angeles out of the mayor's office for nearly a decade, "the Combination." And although many authors still credit Benjamin "Bugsy" Siegel with kickstarting the City of Sin, it is the remnants of this Spring Street clique of gamblers—vice barons like Guy McAfee and Tutor Scherer—that are widely considered the founding fathers of modern-day Las Vegas. But what would Las Vegas be today if these pioneers never left California? Though no doubt backhanded in its delivery, Ed Reid's best-selling *The Grim Reapers* gave at least some of the credit to Jack Dragna and the local brugad. "In any case, many authorities believe that Bugsy was the first one to recognize the mother-lode potential of Las Vegas." Yet, "It was Dragna, however, who unintentionally moved big-time gambling into Vegas when he attempted to 'muscle' into the bookmaking activities in Los Angeles."

Shaving the long-hovering Hollywood conjecture with a blade of fact, *Los Angeles Underworld* allows a fuller and more accurate version of Los Angeles's sordid past to finally surface, revealing a fatalistic reality of a mob era far too often portrayed in over-romanticized fashion. Drawing from personal ties to the subject matter, this work features intimate keepsakes pulled straight from the family albums of key players, and the unseen archives of police detectives directly in the fight against the intricate workings of organized crime. Depicting the City of Angels' assorted illicit rackets through an unparalleled collection, this work showcases the faces and locations earlier authors wrote about but failed to display visually. Here is to the unveiling of a truer *L.A. Confidential.*

Enjoy,
Avi and J. Michael

One

BLACK HANDERS

Heightening a popular misconception about the beginnings of organized crime in America, prior to the coming of Prohibition, newsmen blamed a great deal of criminal activity on the "dreaded black hand." In what can probably best be described as a journalistic black hand craze, the press of the early 1900s vigorously pushed the concept of a nationwide syndicated secret society of Italian conspirators. Fueling these exaggerations and the myth that arose was the reoccurring appearance of a crude drawing of a black hand, which turned up at crime scenes and blotted the pages of threatening letters. Sadly, Italian immigrants did prey upon their own kind, though this segment only made up an exceedingly small percentage of the overall ethnic population. Some of these criminals are viewed today as a precursor to the American Mafia. Though used almost interchangeably with the mafia, the term "black hand" merely describes a set of tactics that had long been employed by crooks and killers of every denomination—arson, extortion, kidnapping, and bombings. Far more likely responsible for the bulk of these crimes were local street gangs and independent miscreants targeting the prospering members of their own communities. The origins and earliest-known use of the image of a black hand for extortion purposes has been traced to Spain rather than the island of Sicily. Once newsmen blamed the Italians, however, extortionists of a variety of ethnic backgrounds purposely adopted the symbol in order to divert the attention of lawmen. The federal files explain, "Some of the extortion cases with Black Hand insignia investigated by the Bureau indicate that Black Hand methods have also been used by non-Italians against non-Italian victims." A prime example is seen in the catastrophic 1910 bombing of the Los Angeles Times Building, an act committed by printer James McNamara. But detectives uncovered something deeper. James and his younger brother John, the secretary of the International Association of Bridge and Structural Ironworkers, were entwined in a nationwide bombing spree undertaken in the name of the union.

On September 30, 1910, newspaper printer James McNamara (below, far left) crept alongside the Los Angeles Times Building carrying a suitcase full of dynamite. He rigged the device for 1:00 a.m.—a time he swore he thought the place would be empty. Instead, 20 employees perished. Those not crushed when the south wall collapsed (above) burned or suffocated once ruptured gas lines ignited broken barrels of printing ink. Spreading fires injured nearly 100. The American Federation of Labor hired attorney Clarence Darrow (seated second from the left), and it soon came to light that James and his brother John were involved in a deep conspiracy. Accomplice Ortie McManigal revealed that James McNamara had been traveling the country with a bombmaker-engineer, taking in $200-plus expenses for each explosion. Turning state's evidence against the others, McManigal, a 39-year-old ironworker and fellow bomber, received a suspended sentence. (Both, Niotta Collection.)

James McNamara delivered two other packages late that evening before fleeing the scene and catching a train for San Francisco. He visited the home of Merchants and Manufacturers Association secretary F.J. Zeehandelaar and also stopped off at the residence of *Los Angeles Times* publisher and general manager Harrison Gray Otis. (Otis is pictured right at center; his palatial estate is below.) Luckily for these influential businessmen, only one bomb went off that evening. Otis's son-in-law had a close call as well. Stepping out of his office for some fresh air moments before the Times Building explosion, assistant general manager Harry Chandler narrowly cheated death. The blast killed the secretary still sitting in his office. The newspaper hired investigators, who made three arrests in April 1911. Detectives picked up two bombers in Detroit and another in Indiana. (Both, Niotta Collection.)

4337   Los Angeles, Cal., Residence of Harrison Gray Otis.

Famed attorney Clarence Darrow and his client, bomber James McNamara, appeared in court during jury selection. The initial group of talesmen gathered appear above. Less than six from this

lot were selected for the task of deciding McNamara's fate. (George Grantham Bain Collection, Library of Congress.)

Although James McNamara confessed, the detective work of William J. Burns (center front, wearing a black trench coat) proved the dynamiter shaved some facts. McNamara claimed ignorance of the gas lines, yet Burns showed that the gas cocks were purposely knocked off. In *The National Dynamite Plot*, a book Ortie McManigal wrote while sitting in Los Angeles County jail, he admits he spent four years destroying property on orders of labor union leaders. Burns, he wrote, convinced him to confess. In the end, over 30 labor unionists went to Leavenworth. Likely because no one was injured during the Llewellyn Iron Works bombing, John McNamara (left) only received 15 years at San Quentin. Upon release, he resumed work as an organizer for the ironworkers' union. His brother James faced life and died of cancer in prison in 1941. John followed two months later. (Both, Niotta Collection.)

In the summer of 1915, wealthy Long Beach businessman Dominic Lauricella received a series of threatening letters. The notes, along with his residence, were ornamented with the usual symbols—drawings of a skull and crossbones, a dagger dripping blood, and life-sized black hands. Not his first time being targeted, Lauricella reported the incident. The police set a trap, and by morning, three suspects sat in jail—would-be brothers Jack and Ben Rizotta and longtime friend of the victim Salvatore "Sam" Streva. Although charges against Ben were dropped, word from an official in Sicily cinched Jack's guilty verdict. Corleone's chief of public surety recognized the suspect from his picture and identified him as Ignazio Dragna, "principal friend" of "an acknowledged leader of the mafia." Found guilty, Judge Craig dished out a three-year sentence. But Jack's insistence eventually warranted a retrial. The loose translation of the extortion letter read in court was deemed a technicality. And so, after serving just six months, Jack "Rizotta" Dragna (top left) received a release. But newer proceedings never occurred, and by October of that year, all charges were dropped. (California State Archives.)

Sam Streva (below) was another matter. Authorities believed him to be the ringleader of an extortion gang operating out of San Pedro. The Rizottas joined him in early 1915, after leaving New York. As it had for Jack Rizotta, correspondence with Italy hampered Streva's ruling. The prosecution uncovered that he had killed a man in Sicily many years back. Worse still, extortion victim Dominic Lauricella (left) had been warned not to appear at the trial. The judge issued a bench warrant to gain his testimony. On the stand, Lauricella revealed that he thought Streva had extorted him for $1,000 back in 1913. The 54-year-old San Pedro rancher served just 14 months of a three-year sentence. Though released before the coming of Prohibition, he would not live to see the drought's end. Streva passed at the age of 65 in 1928. (Left, Niotta Collection; below, California State Archives.)

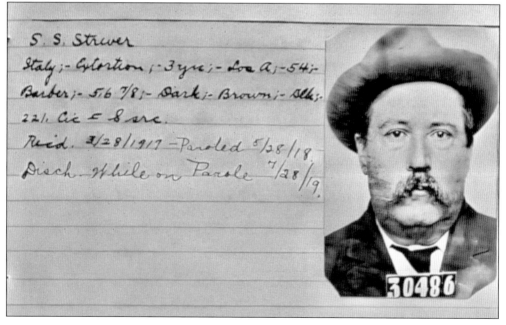

Two

BOOTLEGGERS

When Pres. Woodrow Wilson opposed the idea of Prohibition, Congress circumvented his will, making it an amendment. And when Congress introduced the Volstead Act—the set of rules for navigating Prohibition—the president vetoed and lost that battle, too. But the Noble Experiment failed miserably. FBI files as far back as the 1950s reveal, "the wealth and influence achieved by Mafiosi before 1920 were insignificant compared to what they had achieved by the end of Prohibition. To Mafiosi, the manufacture and sale of illegal liquor was the ring on which they cut their teeth." Local criminals now had a reason to organize and set up national distribution channels, taking their illegal rackets to a grander stage. The 18th Amendment, as the feds also admitted, "endowed the Mafia with fabulous funds and took it from the isolated Italian quarters and bestowed it on the cities as a whole." But in California, the morally based decision stripping Americans of their right to buy, sell, manufacture, and transport alcoholic beverages did more than merely give rise to criminal groups like the mafia—it hampered one of the state's most profitable legitimate industries. California produced over 80 percent of the nation's wine grapes. The City of Angels was even formerly called the City of Vines. While appeals to the president made by these Italian "grape men" proved futile, some found help locally. Nearly a century later, the *Los Angeles Times* elaborated, "When mafia members descended on the foothill communities to purchase grapes to ship back east, they ended up rescuing many small family vineyards, wineries and wine stores that populated Route 66 from San Bernardino to Los Angeles." Ranchers Joe Ardizzone and Jack Dragna—two future local crime bosses—made a bundle brokering deals nationally. Ardizzone's family explained that he boarded trains back east and met with Al Capone and others. But grapes were far from the only moneymaker in the drought. Yet the immense revenues generated from importing liquor by ship, selling medicinal whiskey at pharmacies, supplying speakeasies, and distilling homemade batches spurred violent competition—hijackings, warehouse robberies, and shootouts all erupted over control of the bootlegging rackets.

Catering to wholesale liquor distributors, speakeasies, and bottle dealers, young rumrunner Tony Cornero became a millionaire in his twenties. Employing their sailing skills, Tony, Frank, and Louis Cornero—three brothers who sometimes used their stepfather's last name of Stralla as an alias—carved a profitable niche. They imported liquor from abroad then hid their caches behind Catalina and Channel Islands. Bringing in small loads from ship-to-shore with speedboats let them easily outrun slow and bulky Coast Guard crafts. But a rivalry hatched in June 1925 when Page brothers—Farmer, Ross, and Stanley—hijacked a Cornero shipment (80 cases of imported whisky). Shot in the leg, Cornero gangster Jimmy Fox (alias Jimmy Burns) ended up at Angelus Hospital. A few days later the *Los Angeles Times* reported, "Cornero with revolvers handy" raided a Page warehouse and "took back his own and 320 cases to boot." Next, the Pages went after Tony personally, snatching the 25-year-old gangster off the street. When they held him hostage and threatened to take him for a ride, his brothers promised to return the haul. Instead, they devised a plan. (Bash Collection.)

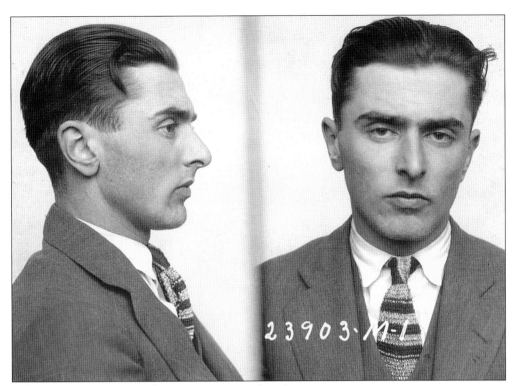

When four Page gangsters drove out to Willowbrook to retrieve their whisky on a stormy night in August 1925, machine gun fire erupted. Police later found pieces of the Browning responsible. "If I live, somebody's going to die," 27-year-old Jake Barrett (Jack Collins) threatened while suffering from four gunshot wounds at Seaside Hospital. Under police guard at Clara Barton, 28-year-old C.H. Munson wore three extra holes himself. Doctors did not expect either to live. A third victim, George "Les" Bruneman (left), drove Munson to the hospital. Showing a charming side the public would come to love, Tony Cornero settled their medical bills. But when Page bodyguard Walter Hesketh (Eddie Egan) turned up dead, officers arrested Tony. Also hauled in as a suspect was fellow gang member Johnny Roselli (above). The Boston transplant turned 20 a month earlier. (Above, John Binder Collection; right, Bash Collection.)

In 1925, James Stanislaus Fox, a Bay Area bantamweight, ended a 25-bout career, came to Los Angeles, and joined Tony Cornero. The pair had growing up in San Francisco in common. When three gunmen tried forcing Fox into a sedan outside the St. Regis Hotel (right) in August 1926, he darted into the lobby. Taking cover, Fox emptied his .25 caliber pistol then fled out the back. Bullet in head, Harry Moran stumbled outside, making it to the hospital before dying. A distance away, H.C. Munson turned up cold in a car. When police asked Fox to identify the bodies, they discovered that Moran belonged to Cornero's crew. Fox wept at the sight of his friend. Perhaps mistaking Moran for Fox, a Page gunman opened fire. Rightly, newspapers blamed bootlegger rivalry. Above, Fox appears at left for an upcoming fight against Johnny Kilbane. (Above, *Oakland Tribune*; right, Niotta Collection.)

When 29-year-old Jimmy Fox turned himself in, headlines read, "Ex-Boxer Admits Killing Los Angeles Gunman." He gave his confession to deputy sheriff Clem Peoples (pictured above with his colleagues, second from right). No love lost for the dead; Fox revealed Harry Munson was the man who put him in Angelus Hospital a year back with a bullet in his leg. The Cornero-Page rivalry ended after Tony's 1926 arrest (pictured below center at a later booking). They were busted while carrying a load from Canada and Germany. Managing to escape police custody in transit, Tony fled the country. After resurfacing in 1929, he pled guilty to rumrunning charges. When the judge asked why he finally turned himself in, Tony replied, "I love California. I want to live here." In 1931, after serving two years at McNeil Island, he returned. (Above, Niotta Collection; below, Bash Collection.)

The infamous Page brothers got an early start in the Los Angeles rackets. Going from newspaperboys to gamblers under the tutelage of bookmaker-king Zeke Caress, officers were already arresting them for gambling charges before the nineteen-teens. The youngest of the lot, Milton "Farmer" Page (pictured above during a 1935 grand jury trial), became the group's leader. And the Corneros were not the only gang they had scrapes with. In February 1925, Farmer turned himself in for the killing of 24-year-old gambler Al Joseph, a Bay Area bootlegger from the Spud Murphy gang. Farmer explained to authorities that Joseph was a former employee, and that after an argument grew heated, he fired in self-defense. Coming to Farmer's aid was a fellow syndicate member, cocky bootlegger-pimp Albori "Albert Black" Marco. Marco cleared Farmer of the crime when he offered police a pistol and swore it was in Al Joseph's hand. Farmer later partnered with Tutor Scherer in a pair of popular gambling ships, the *Johanna Smith* and, later, the *Rose Isle*. (*Los Angeles Daily News* Negatives, 10216.)

The Dragnas relied on ships as well, but as bootleggers, they also invested in distilling whisky and brandy. Blood and marriage strengthened their operations, which included the Old Henry Ranch near Walnut with its 500 acres, a vineyard, and stables. Jack Dragna is pictured on the family ranch standing far left above his young son Frank Paul. Raw materials vital to the manufacture of liquor at the still sites hidden throughout the Southland came to the Dragnas by way of a wholesale grocery belonging to Big George Niotta. This entrepreneurial gambler, pictured center (in white) in the photograph at right, had a warehouse at 735 Kohler Street. Niotta's youngest son, Steve, later married Jack Dragna's only daughter, Anna. The business, which provided bootlegger stills with sugar, yeast, vats, and metal cans, was overseen by Joe Ardizzone's cousin Frank Borgia. Their remote stills situated in the Mojave and Southern Nevada ran off generator power. (Both, Niotta Collection.)

Pictured on the Dragna ranch are brothers Tom (far left) and Jack Dragna (horseback) with bootlegger friend and fellow brugad member Pasquale "Patsy" Vasta (wearing a black shirt and vest). When dry agents raided in 1923, they found their targets napping. But as the *Los Angeles Times* boasted, someone was awake: "Mrs. Julia Dragna, wife of Tom Dragna, who operates the ranch, fiercely resisted." Julia clubbed several deputies over the head before being overpowered. Agents overturned a 100-gallon still, ten 500-gallon vats of mash, two tons of cracked corn, three of sugar, and seven five-gallon cans all set to transport. Several revolvers and five 30-30 rifles with dum-dum bullets were also confiscated. Officers estimated the operation cranked out 10,000 gallons a day and sold to the consumer at $4 a pint. They even printed cards advertising 170-proof white corn whisky of excellent grade. At the Pomona jail with the Dragnas sat Carmelo Sciortino, Jimmy Costa, Patsy Vasta, Gaspar Scibila (alias of Detroit mafioso Gaspar Milazzo), Joe and Frank Gallina, and Mario Augustino. Suffering a gut wound, Giuseppe Bonventre remained at the ranch. (Niotta Collection.)

Raids proved costly. A second ranch bust claimed 2,775 gallons of wine, and in a garage compartment at Jack's residence, police uncovered another 755 gallons. Nabbed at a Tehachapi still, Tony Bruno, Tony Trapini, and Harry Murray received six months, while Sam Bruno faced life for kidnapping during a truck hijacking. Bootleg–front business Yucatan Products proved unlucky for Tom Dragna (right) and Patsy Vasta. Police arrested them there with five bombs and 5,000 gallons. (Niotta Collection.)

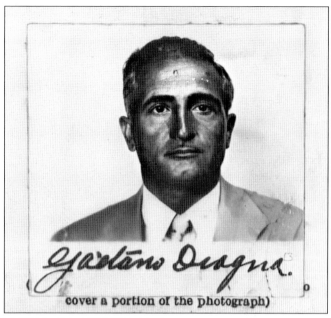

cover a portion of the photograph)

The *Los Angeles Times* assumed every Dragna in Los Angeles was related and even falsely called Jack and Eddie brothers. New York born in 1910, Eddie Dragna—pictured in 1935 with his wife, Ann, and dog Lobo—was 20 years younger. In 1934 he got busted hauling Jack Dragna's untaxed liquor from Nevada. A good friend till the end, the milkman with the Golden State Dairy even helped carry Jack's coffin. (Courtesy of Paulette Dragna-Gainor.)

Adept at avoiding jail were George Niotta's son-in-law Johnny Cacioppo (left) and his brother Gasper—runners (alcohol delivery drivers) for the Dragnas. Hitting a North Broadway warehouse in September 1933, police grabbed Johnny with George Harmon, Angelo Todisco, Frank Allen, Willard Strain, and Johnny Dean. At the trial, the prosecution revealed Cacioppo had six aliases, eight prior arrests—two felonies reduced or dismissed—and a conviction of two misdemeanors (liquor possession and interfering with an officer). Although district attorney Buron Fitts's public enemy crackdown demanded a $50,000 bail, Johnny's lawyer bargained it to $2,500. The *Los Angeles Times* marveled "for the first time since the city and county" began "to arrest gangster suspects under the blanket indictment," someone "jailed under this plan succeeded" in "having his bail reduced to a sum which he could furnish." (Both, Niotta Collection; Cacioppo brother pistols photographed by Belgium Lion Photography.)

On December 12, 1927, when Al Capone and his family stepped off a train into Los Angeles, word spread fast, and the press came running. Also in tune was the Los Angeles Police Department (LAPD), who met Capone at the Biltmore Hotel. When police called for Big Al's exit, Johnny Roselli allegedly offered up his residence. But Capone had enough, complaining, "I just came here for a little rest." By the evening of the 13th, he and his entourage had vanished. Though Capone's next stay out west in 1934 would be Alcatraz, an informant divulged some Angelenos paid him an earlier visit: "Numerous interfamily killings were taking place" around 1928 and "peace talks were called by CAPONE," suggesting Capone had invaded. The source—likely Frank Bompensiero—accompanied boss Joe Ardizzone and Jack Dragna to Chicago and later relayed to feds: "CAPONE suggested to DRAGNA that he get an early train back to Los Angeles and wait for ARDAZONE to return on the train and *hit* him when he got off." In this previously unpublished image, Al playfully swings a shotgun at a pal during a 1944 Wisconsin hunting trip. (Bash Collection.)

The *Los Angeles Examiner*'s interview with Capone made it seem like police chief James "Two Guns" Davis had an impact. Davis (standing left, addressing his men) won the 1932 US pistol championship left- and right-handed. Allegedly, his welcoming party gave Al 12 hours to split. But Capone was not the only Chicagoan to invade. Dominic DiCiolla's gang landed the year prior. It has been speculated he came on Capone's orders. (Niotta Collection.)

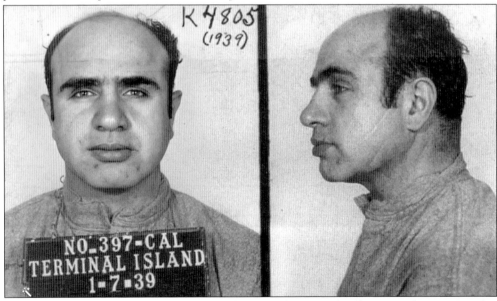

In January 1939, following his release from Alcatraz, Al Capone finally returned to Los Angeles. His contempt of court charge was set to run concurrently with charges of tax evasion. He spent much of the year imprisoned at Terminal Island near San Pedro. According to Jack Dragna's daughter, Anna, Capone's wife and son, Mae and Sonny, stayed as guests at the Dragna residence in Leimert Park. (Terminal Island Prison.)

December 1, 1969

NAME: ANTONIO (NMN) BRUNO
(OO: Los Angeles)

ALIASES: Antonio Bruno, Tony Bruno,
Toni Bruno

DESCRIPTION: Born 8-2-96; San Guiseppe,
Palermo, Italy; 5'11"; 180
pounds; brown hair; blue eyes;
olive complexion; Italian alien;
Registration # 554-0319.

Photo taken 1940

CRIMINAL ASSOCIATES: Jack L. Dragna, Joe Ardizzone (both deceased), John Roselli.

LOCALITIES FREQUENTED: Residence: 431 El Camino Drive, Beverly Hills, Calif.

TRAVEL HABITS: Drives automobile.

CRIMINAL HISTORY: FBI # 500 239; several arrests 1929 to 1935 in connection with bootlegging activities. No criminal arrests since 1935.

FAMILY BACKGROUND: Father - Domiano Bruno (Deceased); Mother - Prudence Bruno, nee LaPuma; Wife - Carmela, formerly Mrs. Joseph Mazzola.

Johnny Roselli's interaction with Capone at the Biltmore Hotel and the fact that he spent a few weeks in Chicago before settling in Los Angeles in late 1923 have led crime writers to assume he was a member of the Chicago Outfit. During the Kefauver hearings, he testified meeting Capone at the Dempsey-Tunney fight in Chicago in September 1927, just three months before Al's Los Angeles visit. Although out an employer following Cornero's 1926 disappearance, an earlier arrest suggests Roselli had already reconciled with the local Italians, and perhaps even joined their ranks. In 1925, dry agents hit Tony Bruno (above) with transporting and vagrancy charges after spotting a jug of wine in his coupe parked near his 843 ½ North Broadway residence. Police returned in 1927 and discovered a hidden plant beneath the floor of his bathroom. When Officers Howard, Kearney, Anderson, and Gibson threatened to shoot their way in, Tony emerged with his hands high. Also arrested on the property were Lorenzo Clemente and Johnny Roselli (under the alias Jimmy Hendrix). (Brendel Marnix Collection.)

HOTEL Sir Francis Drake
*San Francisco's Most
Famous Host!*

The feds learned that during the 1920s, Roselli's closest friend was Johnny Burns—fellow Cornero gangster Jimmy Fox, also known as James Burns. The pair bootlegged and hijacked together and even robbed a Dragna truck. But an informant advised, "That subsequently ROSSELLI and DRAGNA patched up their differences and became close associates." On October 26, 1931, police arrested them in San Francisco. The *Oakland Tribune* called it an "attempt to 'muscle in' on bay region gambling," stating that "Tony Bruno, 24, and John Russell, 23, two suspected machine-gunners" were "taken into custody." FBI files clarify Bruno, Roselli (under alias Russell), Jack Dragna, and Jimmy Costa faced vagrancy charges after police spotted their three revolvers at the Hotel Sir Francis Drake. But the lot also carried permits signed by Los Angeles sheriff William Traeger (standing far left near his replacement, Eugene Biscailuz, beneath the calendar). (Left, Niotta Collection; below, *Los Angeles Times* Photographic Archives, uclamss_1429_3938.)

Three

RISE OF THE
LOS ANGELES MAFIA

Rivalries among Italians in early Los Angeles splintered hope of a collective might. The Ardizzone-Matranga vendetta went all the way back to a 1906 slaying. Although bloodshed carried over into the bootleg era, unification of these warring clans did begin to take shape after the arrival of two high mafia powers—Vito Di Giorgio and Rosario DeSimone. Confiscated letters between Di Giorgio and an imprisoned New York boss named Giuseppe Morello have spurred some to believe Di Giorgio was purposely dispatched to California. Although he did not wear the title of boss long, the 1923 raid on the Dragna ranch suggests his vision touched reality. The mafia don had been dead over a year when eight bootleggers entered the Pomona jail. As The *Pomona Bulletin* reported, the day they landed, $50,000 in cash followed. "The bond in each case was signed by two wealthy Los Angeles Italians, who, it is alleged, have been going on bonds for Italians in such trouble all over this section of country." Shockingly, journalists identified them as Joseph Ardizzone and Tony Buccola—heads of rival Sicilian clans. With the vendetta quelled, they now stood under a single banner. But this influential pair—and numerous other bootleg kings—were soon eliminated in a power struggle. Numerous crime authors have wrongly speculated that the brugad out west played no part in the Cosa Nostra civil war pitting Giuseppe "the Boss" Masseria against Salvatore Maranzano. And yet, as if a far-off domino triggered, violent murders and disappearances in Los Angeles ominously coincided. Smashing these fabrications are the memoirs of high-ranking mafioso Nicola Gentile. Translation of his *Vita Di Capomafia* indicates the following: "The first to go to the restaurant, which had been chosen by Maranzano, were the representatives of California and the far west, ten in all." The Castellammarese War purged the old boss-of-all-bosses system, trading it in for a governing body and a set of rules for all to obey. Los Angeles Brugad member Johnny Roselli offered the following description: "All families, no matter how big or how small, have separate but equal power . . . these bosses don't have an ounce more power than any other."

The earliest-known boss of the Los Angeles Brugad, Vito Di Giorgio (seated), was born in Borgetto, Sicily, on March 19, 1880, and hit New York in 1905. He accumulated a record in New Orleans as Joseph Caronia. Though described by Nicola Gentile as being feared by mafiosos throughout California, newsmen considered Di Giorgio a wealthy fruit dealer. Feared or not, his reputation did not safeguard him. In July 1921, as the Di Giorgio family returned home to 1017 East Twenty-First Street after a beach outing, an assailant struck. Two slugs entered his leg and a third, his groin. Although this was not the first attempt, like the gunmen who struck his New Orleans grocery five years back, the shooter was unsuccessful. During his recovery, Di Giorgio discussed mafia matters with Gentile, who visited him at the home of Rosario DeSimone. In Chicago, on May 13, 1922, following a mafia meeting in Buffalo, two gunmen entered a barbershop and executed the 42-year-old boss as he sat in a chair awaiting a straight razor shave. (Courtesy of Victor DiGiorgio.)

Downey rancher Rosario DeSimone (right) was born in Salaparuta, Sicily, December 12, 1874, and reached New York in 1905. He came to Los Angeles from Pueblo, Colorado, but likely met Di Giorgio in New Orleans earlier. Suggesting a position of interim status, DeSimone stepped down as boss around 1925, after only roughly two years. Perhaps he feared a similar fate. Following a coronary, he passed on July 15, 1946. (Niotta Collection.)

RICH VINEYARDIST STRANGELY MISSING

Joe E. Ardizonne

Born November 19, 1884, Piana de Greci native Joe Ardizzone (left) was just 21 when he fled California after shooting George Maisano. Though acquitted in 1915, the Matrangas did not forget. His tenure was marked by numerous incursions. As Dragna told Capone, boss Ardizzone ordered "many killings for very little reason," though refinement showed while dining with congressmen. After two attempts on his life, Ardizzone retired then disappeared for good in October 1931. (Niotta Collection.)

Church records confirm that Ignacio Dragna was born in Corleone on April 18, 1891, and baptized the following day. His family reached New York when he was seven but returned a decade later. After fighting a war in Africa with Italy's cavalry, "Jack" rejoined his brother Tom stateside in March 1914. Before coming west, the Dragnas worked as drivers in a Harlem laundry with later mob boss Gaetano Reina. The Dragnas befriended another future leader there as well. Tommy Lucchese lived down the street from their East 106th Street tenement. The relationship proved vital. Jack hit Los Angeles early in 1915 and soon engaged in extortion. As boss, he forced where predecessors shied, moving on the rackets of Spring Street gamblers. The Crime Commission stated, "Stick up men raided the books" of McAfee and Scherer and "soon the Italians were cut in!" Taking a cue from the competition, Dragna moved into politics and backed Franklin Shaw for mayor. Despite the rumor of heroin involvement, FBI files convey a strong opposition to narcotics. An informant even advised that he went to New York and complained to the commission about the Tijuana border being used for trafficking purposes. (Niotta Collection.)

Assuming control after the commission's formation meant leading a different Cosa Nostra altogether. Incursions were no longer accepted. And while authors swear the Los Angeles mafia was not on syndicate blotters until they "sent" Bugsy Siegel, an earlier mob summit proves different. The 1932 passenger list (right) of those flying to San Diego after a week at Agua Caliente names the following gentlemen of repute: New York Commission member and boss Vincent Mangano; Joe Bonanno's underboss Angelo Caruso; Cleveland boss Frank Milano; and representing Jewish syndicate interests, Meyer Lansky–Ben Siegel associate Phil Kovelick (below, second from right with fellow Murder, Inc., members). Jack brought two of his own, Jimmy Costa and Johnny Roselli (under alias Jack Russell). Given the proclivity for aliases, other top men may have attended. Below Kovelick's name sits L.W. Smith of Chicago. (Right, Niotta Collection; below, Bash Collection.)

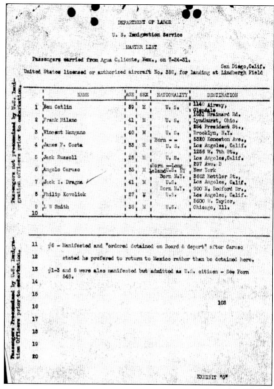

DEPARTMENT OF LABOR

U. S. Immigration Service

MASTER LIST

Passengers carried from Agua Caliente, Mex., on 7-24-31.

United States licensed or authorized aircraft No. 386, for landing at Lindbergh Field San Diego, Calif.

	NAME	AGE	SEX	NATIONALITY	DESTINATION
1	Ben Catlin	39	M	U. S.	1140 Airway, Glendale
2	Frank Milano	41	M	U. S.	1261 Brainard Rd., Lyndhurst, Ohio.
3	Vincent Mangano	40	M	U. S.	254 President St., Brooklyn, N.Y.
4	James F. Costa	33	M	Born -- U. S.	5330 Kenmore Ave., Los Angeles, Calif.
5	Jack Russell	25	M	U. S.	1256 W. 7th St., Los Angeles, Calif.
6	Angelo Caruso	35	M	Born - Long Island U.S.	297 Ave. B New York
7	Jack I. Dragna	41	M	Born N.Y. U.S.	3662 Nettler St., Los Angeles, Calif.
8	Philip Kovelick	27	M	Born N.Y. U.S.	900 N. Bedford Dr., Los Angeles, Calif.
9	L W Smith	38	M	U.S.	5600 W. Taylor, Chicago, Ill.
10					
11	#6 - Manifested and "ordered detained on Board & deport" after Caruso				
12	stated he prefered to return to Mexico rather than be detained here.				
13	#1-3 and 8 were also manifested but admitted as U.S. citizen - See Form				
14	848.				
15					
16					108
17					
18					
19					
20					

EXHIBIT "G"

The *Los Angeles Times* called Dragna (seated between wife, Frances, and daughter, Anna) "the only classic Godfather the city has ever known." His February 23, 1956, death, followed by the suicide of underboss Momo Adamo (left, beside wife, Marie) that summer triggered rapid decline. Learning Marie was unfaithful, Momo shot her in the head then killed himself. Ironically, Marie survived, and her lover Frank DeSimone (below) became boss. DeSimone's selection led to division. Johnny Roselli and Jimmy Fratianno transferred to Chicago, and Frank Bompensiero tried following. Believing DeSimone incapable, Joe Bonanno even attempted a takeover. The son of former boss Rosario DeSimone was born in Pueblo, Colorado, July 17, 1909, and earned a law degree from the University of Southern California. He remained boss for a decade, staying distant from his men until his death of a heart attack in 1967. (Above, Niotta Collection; below, Bash Collection.)

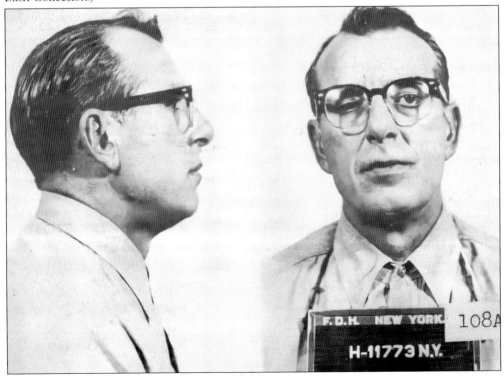

Nicola Licata (right), born in Camporeale, Sicily, February 20, 1897, reached America in 1913 and joined the Michigan mafia group known as the Detroit Partnership. But after offending high-ranking member Joe Zerilli, Licata fled to California, where he befriended Tom Dragna. As consigliere, Tom grew accustomed to listening to members' problems. After the Dragnas smoothed the matter over with Detroit, they allowed Licata to transfer. He long remained in their debt. Licata finally restored his good standing nationally in 1953, with the arranged marriage of his son, Los Angeles member Carlo Licata, to the daughter of Detroit boss Bill Tocco. Nick Licata became boss in 1967, but his health became an issue. Making matters worse for the brugad, underboss Joe "Dip" Dippolito (below) also grew ill. Licata passed October 9, 1974. A heart attack took Joe Dip nine months earlier. (Both, Bash Collection.)

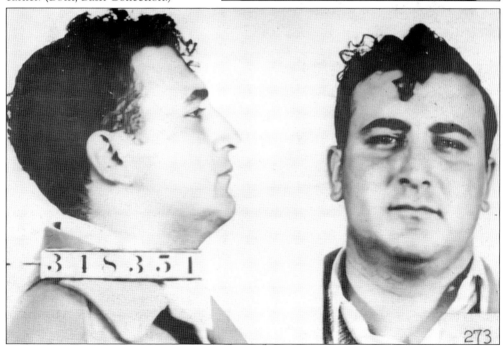

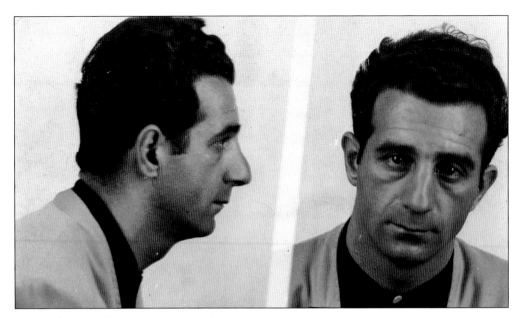

Above, Aladena "Jimmy the Weasel" Fratianno poses for a police mugshot in 1947, the same year as his Los Angeles Brugad induction by boss Jack Dragna. Fratianno's recollection of the ceremony indicates roughly 50 mafioso were present when he and five others were made into the family. In the room he entered where Dragna pricked his finger to draw blood and spoke a Sicilian incantation, Fratianno found a dagger and a revolver overlapped on the table. Dissatisfied with the new leadership following Dragna's passing, Fratianno transferred membership to the Chicago Outfit. But he returned to Los Angeles in 1975 after being offered a leadership position. The opportunity arose when boss Dominic "Jimmy Regace" Brooklier (below) and underboss Sam Sciortino were sentenced to prison on racketeering charges. Jimmy accepted the role of acting underboss beneath the newly appointed acting boss, Jack Dragna's nephew Louie Tom Dragna. (Both, Bash Collection.)

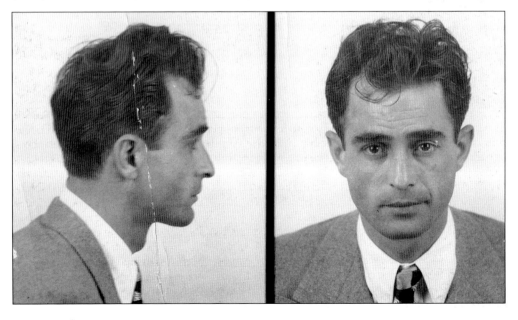

As nephew to boss Jack Dragna and son to former consigliere Tom Dragna, many believed Louie Tom Dragna was groomed for leadership. A Native Angeleno, he was the only Los Angeles boss actually from Los Angeles—even if he only wore the title in an acting status. Fratianno's role as Louie's acting underboss proved to be a mixed bag. Informant Los Angeles T-1 advised, "LOUIS THOMAS DRAGNA continues as acting boss" and "is concerned about JIMMY FRATIANNO's current legal problems and feels that FRATIANNO will have everyone in jail if he continues his current activities." But Jimmy was also unhappy. "FRATIANNO mentioned that he was disenchanted with the lack of activity on the part of DRAGNA," complaining that "DRAGNA had to clear everything through his father, TOM, who is quite elderly." More businessman than gangster, Louie did well with his million-dollar Roberta Manufacturing, a women's garment company in Rosemead at 3330 North San Gabriel Boulevard. His reign ended with Brooklier's return, but the boss saw another conviction late in 1980. Don Brooklier passed in 1984 while serving time in Tucson, Arizona. (Niotta Collection.)

Dominic Brooklier's death left authorities speculating, but they soon found out that Peter Milano took over and appointed his brother Carmen underboss. Mob royalty, their uncle Frank Milano and father, Tony, (left) previously ran the mafia in Cleveland, where Peter was born on December 22, 1925. When the taxman pursued Frank Milano, he turned over control of the Cleveland family and retired to Mexico. In the mid-1940s, Tony Milano relocated closer to his brother, situating his family in Hollywood and then Beverly Hills. Moving to Los Angeles as a young man, Peter Milano quickly befriended the children of other local Cosa Nostra members. Because their community was so tight-knit and closed off to outsiders, interfamily marriages often took place. In 1948, a young Pete Milano (below) and Momo Adamo's stepson Paul ushered at the wedding of Jack Dragna's only daughter. (Both, Niotta Collection.)

NAME: PETER JOHN MILANO
(OO: Los Angeles)

ALIAS: Pete Milano

DESCRIPTION: * Born 12/22/25, Cleveland, Ohio;
5'11", 175 pounds, medium build,
brown eyes, brown hair.

*Photo taken 8/23/76

CRIMINAL
ASSOCIATES: * Samuel Orlando Sciortino; Raymond "Rocky" DeRosa; Dominic Phillip
Brooklier, Dan DeSantis, Louis Thomas Dragna, James Testa,
Aladena T. Fratianno, Winfield Scott Husted, Eugene Williams, aka
Raymond Tyson, Luigi Gelfuso.

LOCALITIES
FREQUENTED: * Residence: 3355 S. Allegheny Court, Westlake Village, California,
and resently purchased condominium at 12 La Cerra Circle,
Rancho Mirage, California; Winfield Trading Co., 5755 Valentine
Street, Ventura, California.

TRAVEL
HABITS: Does not travel extensively. Makes occasional trips to Las Vegas
for pleasure and to Cleveland, Ohio, to visit relatives.

CRIMINAL
HISTORY: * FBI # 282 730 M5. On 4/9/75 pled guilty to one count RICO in USDC,
Los Angeles; on 5/16/75 pled guilty to Federal Narcotics charge
originating in Honolulu; on 6/16/75, sentenced to four years custody
of the AG concurrent with Narcotics and concurrent with four year
sentence imposed for IGB violation on 10/23/74. Started sentence
6/27/75 and was released on parole during March, 1978. Parole
expired 12/17/78.

In 1978, Jimmy Fratianno identified Peter Milano as a *caporegime* (captain). When Brooklier went back to prison, Milano became acting boss and then took over after the godfather's passing. He selected Jack Lo Cicero as consigliere and promoted Palm Springs loan shark Vincent "Jimmy" Caci to "capo." At the helm, Milano became the first boss to push forward in years. The *LA Times* reported that he "presided over a major attempt to recruit new membership" and "extend the family's influence." FBI affidavits revealed efforts "to force bookmakers" to pay "a share of their proceeds," negotiate "tribute payments from narcotics dealers," and he even promised Hollywood they "could deliver labor peace." But a 1984 raid on 22 bookie houses spread throughout the Inland Empire, and Ventura, Los Angeles, and San Diego Counties curbed Milano's play for Los Angeles's million-dollar-a-week bookmaking operation. Police arrested 20 brugad members and confiscated nearly $25,000. Although 1988 delivered a six-year sentence, Milano saw parole in 1991. The Westlake Village resident passed at 86 on April 21, 2012. Peter Milano is the last-known boss of the Los Angeles Brugad. (Marnix Brendel Collection.)

With help from Chicago Outfit boss Frank Nitti, George Browne (left) and Willie Bioff took control of a union representing movie studio stagehands in Chicago. Browne ran for president of the International Alliance of Theatrical Stage Employees (IATSE) in 1932 but lost. To secure the 1934 election, Nitti contacted Murder, Inc., head Lepke Buchalter to ask for Charlie Luciano's help locking in the Eastern vote. Gangsters convincingly pushed delegates to support Browne at the IATSE's Louisville, Kentucky, convention and elsewhere, ensuring his win. (Bash Collection.)

Willie Bioff (right) later testified that he became Browne's assistant in 1932 and began making trips to New York as a union agent in 1935. On business there, he met the Schenck brothers—Nick, president of Loew's, Inc., and Joe, a United Artists president and corporate executive, at the newly formed Twentieth Century Fox. (Bash Collection.)

42

During his 1941 testimony, Willie Bioff alleged that Nick Schenck asked him to deliver a large sum of cash to his brother Joe out west. Joe Schenck left for California after his 1934 divorce to silent-film star Norma Talmadge. Centering in the Palm Springs Movie Colony, he built an estate at 346 East Tamarisk Road in 1935. Joe Schenck is pictured (above) graciously handing a million-dollar charity donation to President Roosevelt. Following the money, Bioff and Browne decided to take their plot to the hub of entertainment. By the summer of 1936, Bioff was already widely known as the big boss in Hollywood. Overseeing Chicago's interests were Paul Ricca (left), Louis Campagna (right), Nick Circella, Phil D'Andrea, and Charles "Cherry Nose" Gioe. The setup worked well until Joe Schenck faced income tax fraud and perjury charges, causing the whole scam to unravel. (Above, Niotta Collection; right, Bash Collection.)

MOVIE STRIKERS PICKET THEATRES

Acme Photo   Timely Events, Inc.

HOLLYWOOD, CALIF. As the strike of Hollywood movie studios set decorators entered its 24th week, the strikers, reinforced by other locals, began mass picketing in front of two Hollywood theatres recently. Here, 10-year-old Frances Cutter leads a parade of lightly clad pickets in front of Warner's, Hollywood.

During a 1936 New York meeting between studio executives and union leaders, Bioff told Nick Schenck and others to approach "heads of the companies and get a couple of million dollars together," or "the industry would have a strike on its hands." Bioff threatened, "We'd close every theater in the country." He estimated his demands to the jury, saying "between two and three million." Bioff and Browne split a third, and the rest went to Paul Ricca to deliver. Joe Schenck's name appears on picket signs on this union mailer. By 1939, Bioff represented 11 Hollywood locals and met with executives like MGM's Eddie Mannix, discussing union pay and working conditions. They again threatened a nationwide strike. By 1940, the IATSE had become the most powerful union in the entertainment world. Bioff hit Warner Bros., Twentieth Century Fox, and Paramount executives, demanding installments as high as $50,000 annually. But Willie got called back to Chicago that year over a 1923 pandering charge. And after returning West, he faced further obstacles. In May 1941, accusations of extortion hit. (Niotta Collection.)

Chicago's extortion of Hollywood has fueled impressions of a weak Los Angeles family. But the outfit's scheme did not originate in California. Back east, Nitti contacted Lepke and Luciano for help. Expanding west, he approached Jack Dragna for assistance. Conveniently, Dragna soldier Johnny Roselli was already in the industry. Roselli's files indicate "the closest man to ROSSELLI was JACK DRAGNA." In 1937, newsmen called Roselli a "former bodyguard for a motion picture executive." Later reports dubbed him a "Hollywood labor investigator" and "assistant film producer." Clarifying, labor conciliator Pat Casey employed him as a representative, but Bioff testified that Roselli also went on the IATSE payroll under the name McCarthy in 1936. Fearing implication, Roselli enlisted in the Army (pictured in uniform with attorney Otto Christensen). But authorities pulled him back after Bioff divulged accomplices. Years later, attorney Ralph Frank told the feds he took a car ride with Roselli in 1943, shortly before Roselli's prison sentence. "Roselli stopped and got out and met with Jack Dragna." They "walked up and down the sidewalk for a few minutes talking" then separated. (Bash Collection.)

Pictured are members of the Federated Motion Picture Crafts on strike in Hollywood in May 1937, not long after Bioff and Browne landed. Under Bioff's grip, the A, F, and L movie unions demanded a 10 percent bump or a theater shutdown. Aided with gangster manpower, they bared their teeth and soon tapped big producers and union coffers, siphoning members' dues at about $60,000 a month. (Niotta Collection.)

Not too keen on prison, Frank Nitti committed suicide after Bioff's confession. Although 38-year-old Johnny Roselli and the rest received 10 years, Roselli's ill health granted his parole in 1947. Probation records state Bryan Foy hired him as an assistant purchasing agent with Eagle Lion Studios. Off the books, he went back to Jack Dragna. Bioff's gruesome end came in Tucson, Arizona, on November 4, 1955, when his pickup exploded. (Bash Collection.)

Four

POLITICAL CORRUPTION

From real estate scams to bootlegging endeavors, brothels, and gambling dens—every mayor in Los Angeles during Prohibition dabbled in some manner of vice. Proceeds from the take that beat cops accepted as tribute from illegal operators steadily filtered upwards into the pockets of Mayor Meredith "Pinky" Snyder. But the setup came to an end in 1921 when George E. Cryer won out in the polls. Cryer is best known as the puppet mayor who did the bidding of a political crime syndicate. The press and crime authors have dubbed them the Combination, the Capitol Hill Gang, the Spring Street Gamblers, and other monikers. Behind the curtain whispered Cryer's campaign manager, University of Southern California alumni Kent Kane Parrot, who entered into arrangements with a handful of Los Angeles vice kings. With Charlie Crawford as the go-between, the group had just about every racket sewn up. Despite involvement with Parrot and his associates, author Warren Hull contends Mayor Cryer also conspired with the competition—secret arrangements with Jack Dragna made the pair wealthy off exploitation of city contracts. When Cryer left office in 1929, he took much of the Combination's might. His replacement, the much more pious John Clinton Porter, was no friend to the Spring Street gamblers. Before becoming mayor, he served on the grand jury indicting the syndicate's prostitution and bootleg man, Albert "Black" Marco. Preaching temperance bought Porter the support of religious superpower, "Fighting" Bob Shuler, who smeared Cryer in his magazine. But not even Shuler's blessing could erase Porter's connections to the Ku Klux Klan. Mayor Franklin Shaw stepped in during the summer of 1933, just months before repeal. In Shaw—as Hull also contended—the Italians mirrored the Combination's play with Cryer, securing his election with the ethnic vote. Preferential treatment in city building and food service contracts followed, along with real estate rezoning and other scams. But the setup collapsed in 1938 with Mayor Shaw's controversial recall. And yet, even under an honest mayor, the police still dabbled in corruption. A decade after the Shaw regime came a loud cry for further reform.

Mayor Cryer (second from right) entertains Mexico's secretary of foreign affairs in 1924, the same year a Los Angeles Brugad–owned construction business incorporated. Partnered with Morici in Phillip Morici & Co. were future brugad leaders Joe Ardizzone and Jack Dragna. In 1927, with Ardizzone now the boss, the pair started another construction venture—the Italo-American Welfare Building Corporation, Inc. Avenues such as these were used to exploit city contracts through the mayor's office. (Niotta Collection.)

Ex-congressman and self-described "Bone Dry" Prohibitionist, William Upshaw (left) congratulates Los Angeles mayor John Porter on abstaining from alcohol shortly after his return from a 1931 mayors' convention in France. In honor of Prohibition, Porter refused to toast. But another picture surfaced a year earlier. When the LAPD vice squad raided a private party in the offices of the Italo-American Welfare League—an Ardizzone-Dragna political organization—detectives found their beloved mayor among 300 gamblers and dancers performing lewd acts. (Bash Collection.)

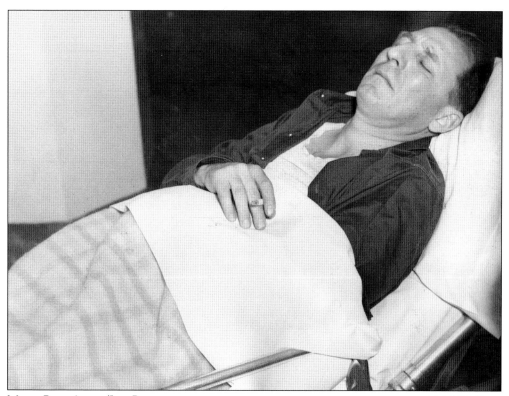

Mayor Porter's son (Lee Porter, secretary and son to the mayor), district attorney Buron Fitts, and police chief Roy Steckel were also seen in attendance, and more than one dancer expressed the event was held in honor of the district attorney. Humorously, Mayor Porter ordered an investigation. Pictured above is Fitts bedridden at the Good Samaritan Hospital with a gunshot wound to his left arm following a 1937 drive-by. After a vehicle pulled beside Fitts on the highway, the shooter unloaded. (Niotta Collection.)

Authors Hull and Druxman indicated that "during Porter's term, Dragna and Frank Shaw engaged in a number of behind the scenes deals which generated a nice income." While not yet mayor, the ethnic vote locked in by the Italian Welfare League secured Frank Shaw's (right) 1925 city council election and his 1928 rise to county supervisor of Los Angeles's 2nd District. The profitable collaboration really blossomed once Shaw became mayor in 1933. (Niotta Collection.)

Under the new mayor, the local brugad continued the practice of securing construction contracts to favored companies. They also pulled real estate scams. After buying useless land at cheap prices, they rezoned the area to allow for businesses to be built then resold the parcels at high dollar, making a hefty profit. Contracts for food vendors providing meals to city-run facilities, such as prisons and hospitals, were also manipulated. They received top dollar for providing aged produce and goods. Serving as a criminal buffer sat the mayor's brother and secretary Joe Shaw, pictured above being released for a four-hour dental session in 1939. Joe dealt directly with gangsters and corrupt members of law enforcement and even controlled the LAPD's hiring and promotions. The Shaw regime filled the police ranks with those who would do their bidding. But this rampant corruption eventually brought on an investigative committee that beckoned for the mayor's recall. Joe Shaw was convicted of 63 out of 68 felony charges related to the falsification of city records and selling of civil service positions. (Niotta Collection.)

More politician than gangster, the "Gray Wolf of Spring Street," Charlie Crawford, sat among LA's most influential. With unmenacing looks and a voice anything but tough, the Spring Street operator's power came from connections in city hall and the ability to fix problems for his racketeer pals. Crawford likely befriended Mayor Cryer's campaign manager, Kent Kane Parrot, at the Maple. This Crawford-owned club on the corner of Fifth and Maple Streets allegedly offered card games and prostitutes. (Niotta Collection.)

Another in the clique was king of the bookies, Zeke Caress, long and well-known among turf-men and bettors at Mexican tracks. A bookmaker even before Prohibition, his run-ins with the law over betting included a 1920 arrest with fellow Spring Street gambler Chuck Addison. Caress's profitable book on Spring Street rested in a bar formerly run by professional boxer Jim Jeffries (above). Tutor Scherer also had a hand in this endeavor. (Bash Collection.)

Also on top of the triangle sat former vice cop–turned–gambling czar, Guy "String Bean" McAfee. Some sources list him as a rival of Charlie Crawford, while others call him a Crawford lieutenant. Whatever the relationship, the two were certainly on the outs toward the end. Although suspended from the force more than once prior, it was in 1917 that McAfee was discharged from the LAPD for running a crap game in the police assembly room. Despite being reinstated into the vice squad, he chose to resign from law enforcement altogether in 1920—just in time for Prohibition. Specializing in gambling endeavors, he headed up bookmaking operations and owned and ran card houses and nightclubs like the Clover Club, which he held with partners Eddie Nealis and Milton "Farmer" Page. In addition to gambling interests, it is alleged that his wife, Marie Conaty, may have been a brothel madam. McAfee's tie-in to prostitution in both Los Angeles and Las Vegas has been strongly suggested, though fellow Combination member and Charlie Crawford associate Albert "Black" Marco was known for heading up that racket. (*LA Daily News* Negatives, b23_22162-2.)

The Spring Street Combination

"Good Time" Charlie Crawford

Guy McAfee

Kent Kane Parrot

Milton "Farmer" Page

Chuck Addison

Zeke Caress

Eddie Nealis

Luther "Tutor" Scherer

Albert "Black" Marco

Mayor George Cryer

Bob Gans

McAfee and Scherer ran two of the city's largest bookmaking operations, and Scherer, who also dealt in real estate, ushered in offshore gambling in Los Angeles and Orange Counties. Club and café owner Eddie Nealis had a number of spots, including the Country Club, Club Casa Nova, and the Century in Hollywood, while the Gans family—Joe, Charles, and Bob—headed up the city's slot machine and mechanical games of chance rackets. Bob Gans later partnered in the Agua Caliente racetrack. Before he took Nealis under his wing at the racetracks, millionaire Zeke Caress nurtured the Pages. These three bookmaker brothers and their gang took to hijacking liquor as well. Albert "Black" Marco also joined the collective. This Italian not among the Italians knew Charlie Crawford from his early Seattle days. The Gray Wolf beckoned him south when he put the syndicate together with Mayor Cryer's campaign manager Kent Kane Parrot. (Niotta Collection, from Niotta's 2018 Las Vegas Mob Museum lecture.)

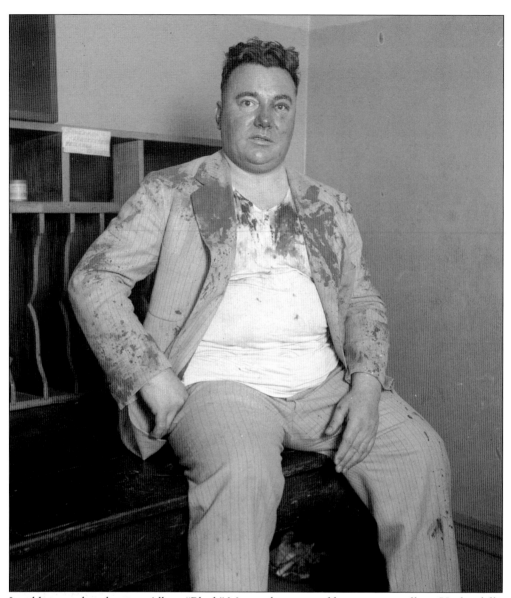

In addition to bootlegging, Albert "Black" Marco also resumed his previous calling. His bordello at 130 South Spring Street was just one of many. Police suspected him of the 1927 slaying of bootlegger Joe Vaccarino, and he faced two counts of assault that same year after shooting Dominick Conterno during an argument in the Ship's Café Venice. "You better watch out," he warned the arresting officers. "I'm Albert Marco, you want to be careful what you do." Marco is pictured in Conterno's blood. While Marco was in jail, August Palumbo tried looking after his rackets, but the competition murdered the bootlegger a month later. Authorities suspected rival Dominic DiCiolla. In 1929, Marco hit the newspapers again, this time in conjunction with Charlie Crawford and Officer Harry Raymond, in a scandal to remove Councilman Carl Jacobson from office. Marco and Crawford were dismissed as defendants that April. Sapping the Combination's power, Mayor Cryer vacated office that year, and the stock market crashed on the October 29. They lost Marco as well. After serving a prison stretch, he found himself deported. (*Los Angeles Times* Photographic Archives, uclalat_1429_b3716_G3047.)

Although the name Gans was huge in New York tobacconist circles, a few members of the family relocated to California. Come 1901, Jonas "Joe" and Charles Gans had a pair of cigar shops on Spring Street as J.J. Gans & Bro. By 1904, Bro. went to Bros., and advertisements listed teenager Robert "Bob" Gans as salesman. Eventually, they entered another industry—one which elevated Bob to the title of slot machine king of Los Angeles. When Cartago shop owners were arrested in 1918 for carrying a Gans machine that paid cash, Charles appeared. Lying to the sheriff, he claimed it had been rigged and then suggested the money be donated. In 1925, while representing the Jennings Mint Vending Company, Charles hit a snag moving product into Santa Barbara. The chief of police pushed back. In the 1930s, they advertised "amusement games" for their Automatic Vendors Company. (Both, Niotta Collection.)

Help Him
BRING BACK PROSPERITY
AND
MORE JOBS

REPEAL the WRIGHT ACT
VOTE YES
on
Number 1
at the election November 8th

The Volstead Act allowed each state to regulate Prohibition independently. When California adopted the Wright Act in 1922, it hit Italians hard, removing their right to make homemade wine. The *Los Angeles Times* explained, "Heads of families in California may no longer make their annual 200 gallon supply of fruit juice which may ferment." Additionally, it gave control of all branches of law enforcement to the district attorney in the fight against bootleggers. (Niotta Collection.)

Under orders of newly appointed Los Angeles district attorney Asa Keyes, dry squad head captain George Contreras (in white hat, standing with Tony Cornero's confiscated slot machine) began an aggressive campaign of rousts on Italian neighborhoods and properties. In September 1923—just three short months after Keyes settled into the position—Contreras led Prohibition agents in a huge raid on the Dragna ranch near Walnut. (Bash Collection.)

In June 1923, health issues forced district attorney Thomas Woolwine to resign, which allowed the morally questionable deputy district attorney Keyes to take over. Italian communities quickly became a favorite target, eventually prompting retaliation. In January 1926, 5,000 Italians rallied in a campaign to drop the Wright Act's harassment. Those pulling the strings wanted to take the power from Keyes's position. Sen. Joseph Pedrotti backed the new organization leading the fight. Coincidentally, he joined the Senate in 1925, the same year the Italian Welfare League set up headquarters on North Spring Street. Chairman Pedrotti's board members included cofounders Ardizzone and Dragna, who incorporated in 1927 with fellow mafia members Rosario DeSimone, Jimmy Costa, and Pietro Matranga. They rallied in January 1926. Come March at Walker's Auditorium, their attorney Griffith Jones explained that Italian homes were being illegally entered by county liquor agents, who insulted and humiliated families. Exemplary of Keyes's tenure, charges of bribery sent him away to prison in 1928. He served 19 months at San Quentin. He is pictured in spectacles shaking the warden's hand upon his release. (Niotta Collection.)

Clifton's Cafeteria, 618 S. Olive Street, Los Angeles, California

Clifton's "Brookdale" Cafeteria
648 So. Broadway, Los Angeles

Mayor Shaw took oath for a second term in 1937, defeating Clifton's Cafeteria chain-owner Clifford Clinton. Although the restaurateur turned politician lost the election, Clinton was far from through with politics and with Franklin Shaw. His cofounded Citizen Independent Vice Investigating Committee (CIVIC) remained determined to highlight corruption—and soon, they did. To do his digging, Clinton hired mysterious figure Jimmy Utley and ousted LAPD cop–turned–private investigator Harry Raymond. CIVIC efforts allegedly uncovered 300 gambling dens, 1,800 bookies, 600 brothels, and police protection. The fingers, it seemed, pointed straight at the mayor's office. But for meddling in vice, Clinton soon tasted retribution, seeing his taxes hiked, smoke bomb attacks on his restaurants, and a slew of food poisoning and trip and fall lawsuits. (Both, Niotta Collection.)

Though Clinton remained unfettered by the costly upset, the approach his attackers took soon became far more direct and dangerous. In October 1937, a bomb erupted beneath his Los Feliz home. Clinton, in his robe, pictured with an officer surveying the damage, received a telephone call shortly after. The caller cautioned the blast was merely a warning. And yet, Clinton still refused to listen. (Niotta Collection.)

Kicked off the force over the Councilman Jacobson scandal, Harry Raymond became a private investigator. But looking into vice for Clifford Clinton proved deadly. On January 14, 1938, Raymond stepped into his Boyle Heights garage and slid into his vehicle. When the key turned, an explosion followed. Surviving over 150 shards of shrapnel, Raymond (pictured with his wife at the hospital) disclosed his investigation of Mayor Shaw's office and corrupt election campaign. (Niotta Collection.)

The bombing trail did not lead to Italian gangsters. Arrested was Earle Kynette (left), chief of Los Angeles's police vice detail, the intelligence squad. Kynette admitted to shadowing Raymond and then implicated Joe Shaw and police chief Davis, alleging they used the vice squad to harass and spy on political opponents. Defending police to the grand jury, Mayor Shaw shifted blame onto police commission vice president Charles Ostrom, stating he represented Farmer Page. (Niotta Collection.)

After handing an oversized wooden key to Superior Judge Fletcher Bowron in September 1938, Franklin Shaw ended his term as mayor. Following this 45-year tradition, Mayor Bowron ushered in a wave of reform, promising the following: "I'm going to break the power these men have. A monopoly has been built up here and the police department has been used to run out competition against those paying for protection." (Niotta Collection.)

Hollywood Hills madam Brenda Allen's discreet pleasure service catered to Hollywood's elite. After being shook down, she grudgingly paid for police protection. Despite assurances, however, authorities raided after policewoman Audre Davis infiltrated as a call-girl. On the stand, Allen divulged her "necessary business expense"— paying up to $150 a week per girl. Her 1948 pandering conviction drew 360 days for lewd vagrancy and operating a brothel. (*Los Angeles Daily News* Negatives, uclalat_1387.)

The police-protected vice scandal blew wide once word of incriminating tapes spread. LAPD sergeant Charles Stoker, who hired a wiretapper, swore to the jury that he turned these recordings over to Cecil Wisdom (right), captain of the LAPD personnel department. Wisdom, who adamantly denied this claim, was later brought up on charges with assistant chief Joe Reed (left) and three others. Ousted, Stoker revealed the corruption in his 1951 memoir *Thicker'N Thieves*. (Niotta Collection.)

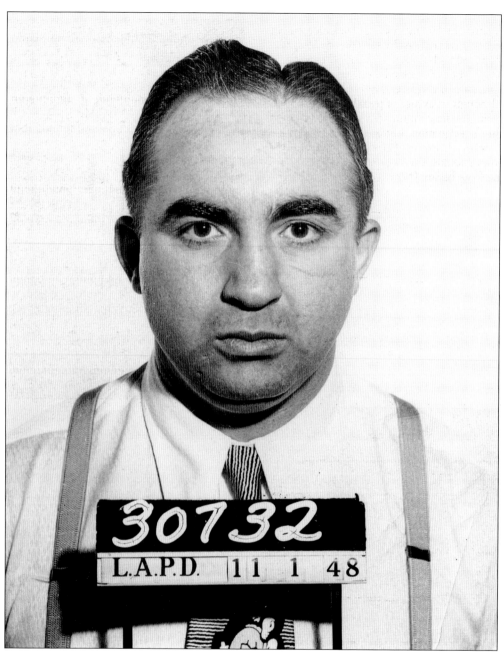

On trial over an unrelated matter, Mickey Cohen seized the opportunity to make lawmen look bad, expressing he too had been a victim of police shakedowns. Mickey personally blamed Brenda Allen's lover, vice squad sergeant E.V. Jackson, and even boasted having recorded proof officers accepted bribes from the madam. Mickey's loud outcry helped bring about a three-month grand jury investigation into police-protected vice, which ultimately plunged a knife in many under-the-table arrangements between crooked cops and criminal operators. As a result, Los Angeles's gambling and bookie establishments severely suffered, and for that, both sides of the law wanted Mickey Cohen dead. The first of several bombings and shootings aimed to snuff the gambler out arrived shortly after. (Bash Collection.)

Among the five members of law enforcement indicted was police chief Clemence Horrall (pictured hatless beside his sheriff escort, Chief Norris Stensland, on their way to superior court to face perjury charges). Although an excuse of poor health was given, the fiasco ultimately prompted the chief's resignation. Just one short decade after the cleansing of crooked Mayor Frank Shaw's administration, another purge of the force began. (Niotta Collection.)

Horrall's temporary replacement, acting police chief William Worton (pictured with a stack of transcripts transposed from a recording device hidden beneath Mickey Cohen's home), drew from his experience as a Marine major-general. Worton warned the public, "I'm going to sift the wheat from the chaff," then announced, "the transfer of four inspectors, two captains, four lieutenants, nine sergeants and 20 policemen." In his first few months in office, he made over 200 transfers. (Niotta Collection.)

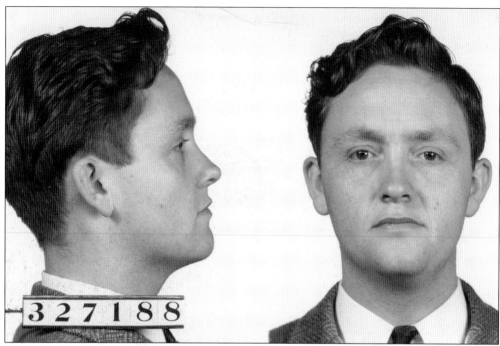

Electronics expert Jim Vaus worked with cops and criminals—though in Los Angeles it was sometimes hard to tell the difference. In 1946, he built bugging equipment for the LAPD, which police used to learn about Los Angeles's bookmaking rackets. Vaus started his double-life soon after, taking a job with Mickey Cohen. Testifying about his part in the bordello shakedown, Vaus stated Sgt. Charles Stoker hired him to set bugs and record conversations. His testimony helped convict Sergeant Jackson, but after finding God with the help of Rev. Billy Graham, Vaas recanted, finally releasing Jackson of false charges. His autobiography admits evidence tampering and giving false testimony to implicate the "innocent police sergeant" to "protect the syndicate." Advertising himself as "Mickey Cohen's Former Henchman," Vaus toured the country, converting followers with his "Christ, Not Crime Crusade." Mickey Cohen was among his biggest supporters. (Both, Bash Collection.)

HEAR

JIM VAUS

FORMER MICKEY COHEN HENCHMAN

AT THE

HADDON HEIGHTS BAPTIST CHURCH

THIRD AND STATION AVENUES, HADDON HEIGHTS, NEW JERSEY

FEBRUARY 17 · 24

SERVICES EVERY NIGHT

WEEKDAYS 8:00 P.M.   SUNDAYS 11:00 A.M. - 7:45 P.M.

Also

Ruth and Bill Ohman

OF THE ORIGINAL " KINGS TRUMPETERS "

" CHRIST, NOT CRIME CRUSADE "

Five

LOS ANGELES'S
FLOATING CASINOS

Although the acclaimed best seller *Five Families* (Selywnn Raab) credits Benjamin "Bugsy" Siegel with the birth of Los Angeles's floating casinos, alleging that Bugsy "added a new wrinkle by launching an offshore casino—on a boat," the venture actually kicked off a full decade before Siegel's West Coast arrival. And although the charming Tony Cornero is typically crowned king of the water gamblers, when the initial wave hit SoCal in the summer of 1927, Tony was nowhere to be found, having fled the country to avoid bootlegging charges. The Spring Street Combination and the local brugad had a hand in the trade long before either personable gangster tested the waters. Lester B. Scherer, or just plain old Tutor, may just be the spark that ignited the offshore craze out west. Eight miles out from Venice Beach, he ushered in the era with his not-so-known and not-so-pretty *Barge C-1*. Situated outside California's jurisdiction, he shouted "immunity" when lawmen shut him down in July 1927. As the *Ogden Standard Examiner* announced on July 27, 1927, gambling den owner Tutor Scherer "took legal steps to prevent official interference with his business, protect his investment in gambling equipment and prevent the sheriff and district attorney from spoiling his reported income of a hundred dollars a week." The profits Tutor refused to report were likely substantially higher. Although he fought the law and went about it the legal route, applying in deferral court for a temporary injunction, in the end Tutor lost the battle. His cries of injustice would be mirrored by just about every owner and operator of a floating casino to follow. The new industry resumed the practice offshore in the summer of 1928 with the coming of the *Johanna Smith,* and Jack Dragna followed that very next season with the *Monfalcone*.

With 38 slot machines, 13 gaming tables, and a fleet of water taxis, the *Johanna Smith* got her start anchored seven miles off Long Beach. Fronting for the Combination was Clarence Blazier. But the *JS* lasted just one season before authorities boarded, seized, and sold her at auction. Using a statute from 1793, county officials called for the forfeiture of the ship, which had engaged in trade she was not licensed for. (Bash Collection.)

Mere weeks after the *Johanna Smith* seizure, one-time Los Angeles bunco king Jim Byrnes gave newsmen a tour of what he called "the finest pleasure barge on the coast." Fellow investor "Doc" Dougherty laughingly admitted that their ship was unregistered, making her immune to the *JS*'s fate. Byrnes ran the dayshift end of the *Monfalcone*'s round-the-clock operation, while Dougherty managed the night. Also listed in newspapers as an original owner was Jack Dragna. (Niotta Collection.)

Below deck in her 200-foot gambling saloon, the *Monfalcone* offered patrons 41 gaming tables, 50 slots, and a high-roller room decorated in blue velvet. On the bow waited another 16 blackjack tables plus eight more just for dice. A third section held additional slots, money wheels, roulette, and chuck-a-luck. Tapped into "Sunny Jim" Coffroth's Tijuana, Mexico, racetrack, offshore gamblers could even place offtrack bets. She greeted patrons in November 1928. (Niotta Collection.)

DINING
DANCING
FISHING

on the Barge

MONFALCONE

off Wilmington

Fast speed boats leave foot of Avalon Blvd., Wilmington, every 30 minutes after 2:00 P. M.

No cover charge.

Shortly after the *Johanna Smith* resumed trade, *Monfalcone* co-owner Nick Oswald sent his attorney to the district attorney's office for help. Oswald, Los Angeles's red-light district king nearly three decades earlier, complained that his partner "Doc" Dougherty and four gunmen had captured the ship. Firing shots in the air, they sent Oswald and Monfalcone Café concessionaire Tommy Jacobs to shore. Humorously, the district attorney's office pointed out the ship was not within California's jurisdiction. (Niotta Collection.)

When a Lincoln sedan failed to stop at Wilshire Boulevard and Vermont Avenue on July 29, 1930, Officers Wolfer and Regur gave chase. As they approached the parked vehicle, they encountered a sawed-off shotgun. But John Canzoneri lowered the weapon at Jack Dragna's request (above right). Johnny Roselli (above left) and James Russo completed the quartet. Newsmen noted that Russo, who claimed to be a *Monfalcone* employee, was the only passenger without a criminal record. But Russo was actually Al Capone's cousin and bodyguard Charlie Fischetti (below). After explaining he co-owned the *Monfalcone* gambling ship and was transporting profits, Dragna produced permits for all but one revolver, saying the firearms were for protection. Although arrested, all but Canzoneri were released after a swarm of character witnesses flocked the station that morning. Canzoneri faced suspicion of assault with a deadly weapon charges. (Above, Niotta Collection; below, Bash Collection.)

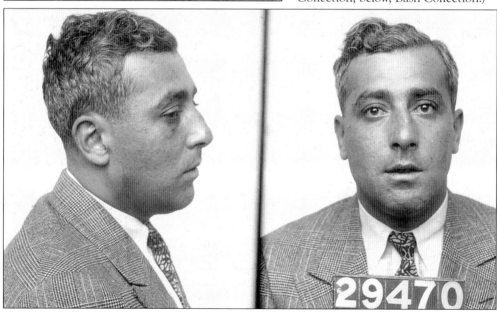

Prior to managing entertainment on the *Monfalcone*, Tommy Jacobs (right) ran the ship's Café Venice (below). As a concessionaire, the former prizefighter looked after the *Monfalcone* pavilion, which offered fine dining, a seven-piece orchestra, and a 125-foot dance floor. But all the fun came to an end abruptly on August 31, 1930, when a leaky generator gas line sparked a fire. Powering the lighting, the outage threw gamblers below deck into darkness. Frantic patrons ran topside, greedy hands grabbed at cash, and one dealer even jumped 40 feet into the ocean. Coat-check girl Lillian Kason returned belongings by candlelight as rescue boats and water taxis ferried folks to shore and to the competing *Johanna Smith*. Jacobs later praised Artzell's Screenland Serenaders, who performed "Happy Days Are Here Again" during the chaos. Spectators watched the *Monfalcone* burn till morning. (Both, Niotta Collection.)

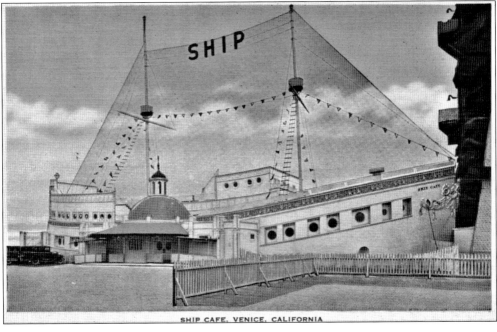

SHIP CAFE, VENICE, CALIFORNIA

It was close to the *Monfalcone*'s two-year anniversary when a generator fire destroyed their investment. Uninsured, the loss was estimated at $115,000. Undeterred, cash quickly spilled into the next venture—a ship with a steel hull. The *Rose Isle*, with her stylish Egyptian motif, filled the empty spot that same year. Unlisted owners included Jack Dragna and Johnny Roselli, who partnered with Tommy Jacobs, Tutor Scherer, and Spring Street gamblers. But the owners soon saw their success hampered by scandals—the kidnapping of Zeke Caress, the murder of an employee, and a police shootout that confined an officer to a wheelchair. In 1932, when the *Johanna Smith* burned to the waterline just like the *Monfalcone*, the owners purchased the *Rose Isle* as a replacement vessel. To shed the gangster reputation, they renamed her the *Johanna Smith II*. (Both, Niotta Collection.)

Tony Cornero entered the popular trade in 1935, introducing the *Tango* (above) with Clarence Blazier. *Life* magazine covered the vessel in a 1937 pictorial. Not big on having a partner, though, Cornero went solo in 1938 after repurposing passenger vessel SS *Rex*. In 1942, however, Los Angeles deputy district attorney Eugene Williams contended that Bugsy held an interest. Reports on earlier gambling ships were less than favorable, so with the *Rex*, Cornero advertised as a straight-shooter. Combatting the stigma, he offered $100,000 cash to anyone who could prove his games were rigged. Like other water gamblers, the *Rex* stayed open around the clock, entertaining thousands of patrons at any given time. But the *Rex* and Cornero faced numerous problems and had more than just Mayor Fletcher Bowron and district attorney Buron Fitts to contend with. Below are invites and casino chips for Cornero's *Rex* and *Tango*. (Both, Bash Collection.)

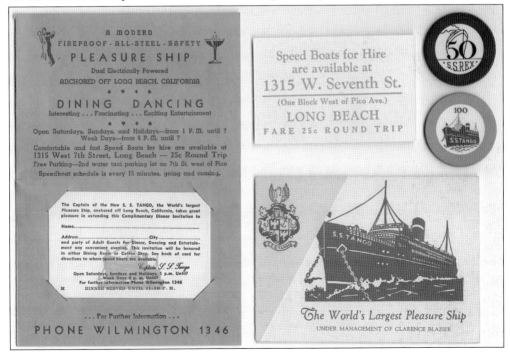

The murder of his 73-year-old father in May 1938 fueled Alameda district attorney Earl Warren's quest for justice. He ran for attorney general that same year and took office January 1939, rising to governor in 1943, and chief justice a decade later. As attorney general (left, shortly after assuming the role), Warren gave floating casinos special attention. The vice squad shut down four in August 1939 and even tossed the roulette wheels of the *Texas* overboard and caused $25,000 in damage. When they hit the *Rex* later that week, Cornero was ready with a high-powered firehose (below). While District Attorney Fitts was never able to make good on threats of taking axes to the *Monfalcone*, George Contreras came close when his smash squad raided the *Rex* that December, ending her tenure. But Cornero defiantly revived the industry after World War II, introducing the *Lux*. (Both, Bash Collection.)

Six

GAMBLERS, BOOKIES, AND THE WIRE

Following Prohibition's repeal at the close of 1933, the FBI quickly noted an almost seamless transition. "Gambling was made to order for them. In gambling—as in Prohibition—criminals offered what many people desired even though it was illegal in many forms. They capitalized on human desires." But as the floating casinos proved out west, several Angelenos were already deeply involved in the gambling rackets. In addition to ships, card houses, and nightclubs, bookies continued to take action on sporting events, including horse racing bets placed offtrack, thanks to a subscription to the wire service. But the struggle for control of racing news proved exceedingly bloody. By the close of the thirties, most of the prominent sportsmen from Spring Street took their leave of Los Angeles, getting settled in Southern Nevada. They had plenty of incentive to leave. Although squeezed by the new syndicate man, Ben Siegel, and tormented by Mayor Fletcher Bowron and Gov. Earl Warren, the most enduring assault on the Combination came at the hands of the Italians, who competed with them in bootlegging and politics then later muscled into their gambling rackets. The Spring Street clique of McAfee, Scherer, Nealis, Addison, and Page would pioneer the Fremont District, having a hand in the Frontier, the Pioneer Club, El Rancho, the Boulder Club, the Golden Nugget, and a variety of other gambling establishments. McAfee is even credited with branding Las Vegas Boulevard "the Strip," after Hollywood's own Sunset Strip. And yet, one trio of Los Angeles brothers gave it a go even earlier. When Las Vegas re-legalized gambling in 1931, longtime Los Angeles operators Tony, Louis, and Frank Cornero made the leap by opening the Meadows. Seeing the potential closer to home, some went a short distance south instead, taking a deeper hold on the horse tracks on the other side of the border. Eddie Nealis invested in Las Vegas with the rest, but he also strengthened his Mexican connection as well, no doubt under the tutelage of bookie king Zeke Caress.

U. S. HIGHWAY 91
LAS VEGAS, NEVADA

TONY CORNERO'S

FABULOUS

tardust

HOTEL AND CASIN

LARGEST AND MOST LUXURIOUS IN THE

Frank Cornero died in a car crash in Las Vegas during the summer of 1941. His brother Louis, who moved to the Napa area in 1933, got involved in the wine industry and became mayor of St. Helena under the name Stralla, passing in 1981. Their brother Tony stuck with gambling. In the mid-1950s, he dreamed up something grand—bringing the glamour of the Strip to the everyday man with the Starlight Hotel and Casino. But the Nevada Gaming Commission refused to grant him a gaming license, complaining he put together too many shareholders. A lot of legwork followed, but Cornero finally bowed out in June 1955. A heart attack took him that very next month while gambling at the Desert Inn. Some say it was foul play. Cornero's project became the Stardust, and his old rival, Farmer Page, sat among those who took over. The Stardust opened in 1958, offering tourists the largest hotel, casino, and swimming pool in all of Las Vegas. Farmer Page passed a couple of years later, dying in his hometown of Los Angeles in 1960. Pictured is an early promotional photograph of the Stardust during construction, still bearing the name of Tony Cornero above the logo. (Bash Collection.)

The old Spring Street clique of political gangsters is well represented at the bottom of this advertisement for the Pioneer Club (right), which opened its doors on Fremont Street in 1942. A decade later, the casino featured the iconic neon sign of Vic Vegas, the smoking cowboy. Before reaching Nevada and becoming a millionaire, Tutor Scherer partook in Los Angeles's bookmaking, nightclub, and floating casino rackets. (Bash Collection.)

Although Wisconsin born, Tutor grew up in Los Angeles following his family's relocation. Well-rounded, he wrote *Reminiscing in Rhyme*, a book of poetry that came out the year before his passing. At left, a camera-shy Tutor is pictured with his third wife, an El Rancho cocktail waitress, nearly a third his age. Sadly, his first wife passed young, leaving him a widower and single father during the late 1920s. Tutor died of a stroke in Las Vegas in 1957. (Niotta Collection.)

REGISTRATION CARD—(Men born on or after February 17, 1897 and on or before December 31, 1921)

SERIAL NUMBER	1. NAME (Print)			ORDER NUMBER
T 202070	EDWARD	GABRICL	NEALIS	T 11850-A
	(First)	(Middle)	(Last)	

2. PLACE OF RESIDENCE (Print)

Hollywood Roosavalt Hotel _____ Hollywood _____ Calif

(Number and street) (Town, township, village, or city) (County) (State)

[THE PLACE OF RESIDENCE GIVEN ON THE LINE ABOVE WILL DETERMINE LOCAL BOARD JURISDICTION; LINE 2 OF REGISTRATION CERTIFICATE WILL BE IDENTICAL]

3. MAILING ADDRESS

Same 21 San Juan De La Tran, Mexico City

[Mailing address if other than place indicated on line 2. If same insert word same]

4. TELEPHONE		5. AGE IN YEARS		6. PLACE OF BIRTH	
		43		Los Angeles	
		DATE OF BIRTH		(Town or county)	
		3 18 1899		California	
(Exchange)	(Number)	(Mo.) (Day) (Yr.)		(State or country)	

7. NAME AND ADDRESS OF PERSON WHO WILL ALWAYS KNOW YOUR ADDRESS

Mrs M. Nealis — Hollywood Roosavalt Hotel

8. EMPLOYER'S NAME AND ADDRESS

Self

9. PLACE OF EMPLOYMENT OR BUSINESS

21 San Juan De La Tran = Mexico City

(Number and street or R. F. D. number) (Town) (County) (State)

I AFFIRM THAT I HAVE VERIFIED ABOVE ANSWERS AND THAT THEY ARE TRUE.

Edward G Nealis.

D. S. S. Form 1
(Revised 1-1-42) (over) GPO 16—21630-1 (Registrant's signature)

As Eddie Nealis's World War II draft card shows, the wealthy gambler kept a Hollywood hotel home for himself and the missus but took his mail in Mexico City. When the racetracks stateside shutdown for use in the war effort, the track at Agua Caliente became the horseracing hub for Californians. Nealis, along with his mentor Zeke Caress, started Caliente's new Jockey Club, which opened in May 1943 with Nealis as club president. Taking on partners, the pair purchased the rights to the track and its races. Nealis then moved up to general manager. Pictured below is Agua Caliente's luxurious Gold Bar casino. Although Caress was an early investor, they both lost out in December 1944 when the Mexican government forced a seizure. Escorted by police, an Arguello family heir took possession. (Both, Niotta Collection.)

184:—INTERIOR OF CASINO AND FAMOUS GOLD BAR.

AGUA CALIENTE, TIJUANA HOT SPRINGS, MEXICO.

Jack Dragna ran faro and poker, starting in the 1930s with cards and dice on East Seventh Street. Poker at Hawthorne's Prairie Club continued into the 1940s. Jack also partnered with Roselli in a short-lived dog track. In 1946, the Dragnas expanded into Las Vegas, purchasing bars and cafés. An arrangement there with Sheriff Glenn Jones freed them whenever police arrested. In 1951, Tom built a ranch in Paradise Valley, and later, Benny Binion (right) gave them 25 percent of the Fremont Casino for disposing of his extortionist, Russian Louie Strauss. Jack opted for installments, and Binion made good, paying for over a decade. A bugged telephone conversation suggests that Jack and Allen Smiley may have owned an interest in the Desert Inn (DI) as well. The brugad spent a lot of time at the hotel and with DI owners Lou Rhody and Moe Dalitz (left). In 1953, Dalitz pulled favors with Ohio's governor, exerting pressure to delay Jack's deportation. Strip operators even raised funds for his bond. In 1955, the Dragnas deposited $15,000 in a Las Vegas bank, allegedly to start a plumbing business. Dalitz and Binion, both considered early pioneers of Vegas, would die within six months of this April 1989 photo. (Bash Collection.)

John Payne left Western Union in the early 1900s to strike it rich, making room for half a century of violence. Staging spotters at tracks who signaled the winners to a nearby telegraph operator allowed him to offer real-time results to bookmakers nationwide. This allowed bookies to avoid "post-betting," taking bets from gamblers who already knew the winners. Distributors received results by teletype then provided them to subscribers via scratch sheets. (Niotta Collection.)

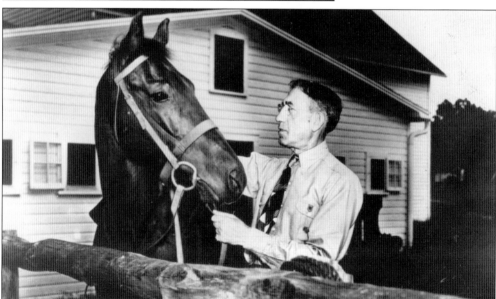

In 1911, after years of subscribing to Payne's service, Mont Tennes opened the Tennes General News Bureau. Come 1927, Tennes was out, and Moe Annenberg (above) partnered. Running General News out of business in 1934 by opening competing service Nationwide allowed Annenberg to dominate the industry. Distributing Nationwide in SoCal was Jack Dempsey's former manager, Gene Normile. In 1936, Normile gave 10 percent to Roselli and the Los Angeles Brugad. But the taxman ended the arrangement. (Bash Collection.)

Around late 1939, Tom Kelly (right) approached Nationwide's former general manager James Ragen Sr. about filling the void left after the taxman forced Annenberg's departure. Attributing Annenberg's success to Ragen's strong-arm tactics, Kelly considered Ragen vital and persuaded him to partner with Arthur "Mickey" McBride in Continental Press. Ragen's and McBride's sons also partnered, and Ragen's son-in-law Russell Brophy even took over Normile's California position, with Russell's brother Leonard overseeing San Diego. (Niotta Collection.)

Years later, Johnny Roselli testified that he briefly served as a consultant for Brophy's *Los Angeles Journal.* On November 16, 1940, the *Los Angeles Times* reported on their partnership, stating "a newly organized racing news service is available to San Diego bookmakers at a charge of $1,000 to $1,500 weekly." The *Times* also highlighted Roselli's arrest with the Brophy brothers. Brophy employee George Redston testified that Ragen (left) put an end to their arrangement. (Niotta Collection.)

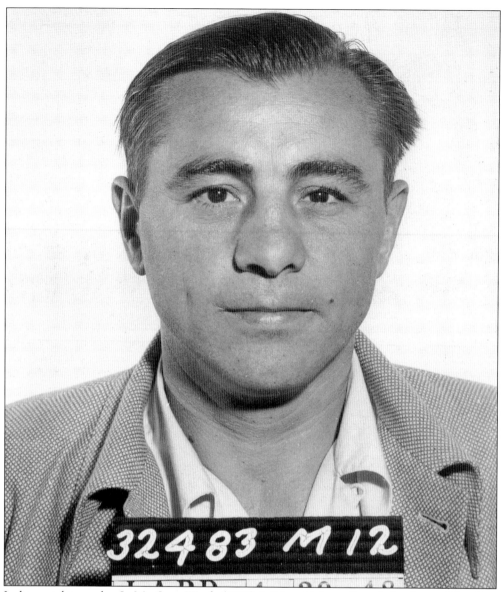

In his autobiography, *In My Own Words* (1975), Mickey Cohen alleged that he and Joe Sica (above) sided with Benjamin "Bugsy" Siegel in a rivalry against Dragna and Roselli, stating that they beat up Russell Brophy and destroyed his Continental offices against the brugad's wishes. But Redston's sworn testimony and coauthored work, *The Conspiracy of Death* (1965), offers a contrasting story. Prior to Brophy's 1942 assault, Dragna—whom Redston described as "very friendly"—called a meeting with Los Angeles's Continental heads and explained he "wanted Mickey Cohen and Joe Sica to distribute Continental's racing sheets." Despite Cohen's contentions and Hollywood's depictions, Dragna and Siegel clearly worked together. Angered with Brophy for accepting Dragna's arrangement, Redston quit then left for Chicago and filled in James Ragen. Joe Sica's 1951 testimony conveyed that—for a time—Brophy complied against Ragen's wishes. "The knock-down fight in Brophy's office," Sica contended, "stemmed from the fact that Brophy had kicked" him "out of his job of distributing race scratch sheets after" he "built up a lucrative clientele." The reversal was Ragen's influence finally taking hold. (Bash Collection.)

Unable to muscle Continental, the syndicate started a competing service. A wiretapped conversation between Dragna and Siegel on September 11, 1946, shows they partnered in Trans-American (TA). Siegel tended to Nevada where gambling was legal, while Dragna handled California. Chicagoan Ralph O'Hara (above) served as secretary. Setting up, Jack incorporated West Coast Publishing to receive TA's racing information. Jack's nephew Louie Tom Dragna worked in its Ferguson Building offices. (Bash Collection.)

Underboss Momo Adamo handled the Santa Anita Track come-back money for Las Vegas bookmakers. The track's turf club is pictured above. When five spotters were arrested and a high-powered telescope confiscated after police raided a TA house set near the track, Jack Dragna did more than install replacements. He fixed matters through the district attorney's office. But the deal did not protect TA's Pico Boulevard location. When the LAPD raided, they destroyed their scratch sheets. (Niotta Collection.)

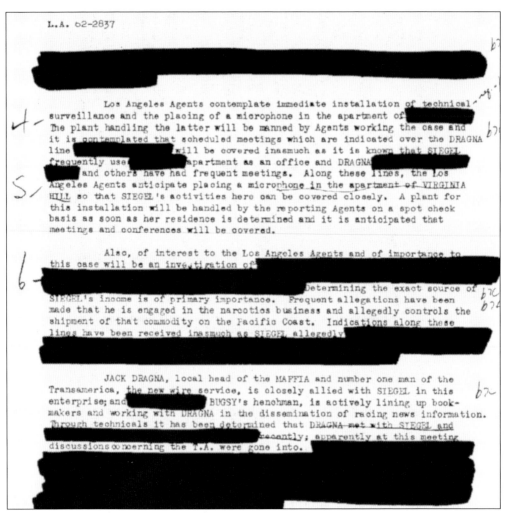

Los Angeles Agents contemplate immediate installation of technical surveillance and the placing of a microphone in the apartment of ▮▮▮ The plant handling the latter will be manned by Agents working the case and it is contemplated that scheduled meetings which are indicated over the DRAGNA line ▮▮▮ will be covered inasmuch as it is known that SIEGEL frequently use ▮▮▮ apartment as an office and DRAGNA ▮▮▮ and others have had frequent meetings. Along these lines, the Los Angeles Agents anticipate placing a microphone in the apartment of VIRGINIA HILL so that SIEGEL's activities here can be covered closely. A plant for this installation will be handled by the reporting Agents on a spot check basis as soon as her residence is determined and it is anticipated that meetings and conferences will be covered.

Also, of interest to the Los Angeles Agents and of importance to this case will be an investigation of ▮▮▮ Determining the exact source of SIEGEL's income is of primary importance. Frequent allegations have been made that he is engaged in the narcotics business and allegedly controls the shipment of that commodity on the Pacific Coast. Indications along these lines have been received inasmuch as SIEGEL allegedly ▮▮▮

JACK DRAGNA, local head of the MAFFIA and number one man of the Transamerica, the new wire service, is closely allied with SIEGEL in this enterprise; and ▮▮▮ BUGSY's henchman, is actively lining up book-makers and working with DRAGNA in the dissemination of racing news information. Through technicals it has been determined that DRAGNA met with SIEGEL and ▮▮▮ recently; apparently at this meeting discussions concerning the T.A. were gone into.

A lot of effort went into readying the new service. In California, where offtrack gambling was illegal, Jack Dragna ran into difficulties. He located and leased properties to serve as bookie houses, purchased teletype and telephone equipment, and hired spotters to take in results from racetracks. As this page from Ben Siegel's FBI files shows, "Bugsy's henchman" Mickey Cohen (name redacted) and Joe Sica assisted Dragna as musclemen with orders to convince subscribers to leave Continental for TA. But shortly after opening, the new service shut its doors for good. After James Ragen told authorities the Chicago Outfit was muscling his service, shotguns blasted. Though the FBI blamed Chicago gangsters, Gov. Earl Warren's crime commission alleged Ragen's last words were "Dragna is the Capone of California." With the McBrides cooperating, the need for Trans-America evaporated. FBI files explain that in June 1947, shortly after TA folded, Leonard Brophy divulged the following: "FRANK BOMPENSIERO was the actual head of Trans-American in San Diego under JACK DRAGNA and [Tony] MIRABILE." Brophy admitted paying the brugad $60 a week per customer. (Niotta Collection.)

Scratch sheets offered results and stats, giving gamblers the impression they had an edge in a game of pure chance. Dragna's Globe Distribution published the Blue Sheet, which provided subscribing bookies with TA's information. But when TA folded, Dragna sold. In 1950, he testified that "business was bad and I turned the scratch sheet over to the Illinois Sports News," who "guaranteed to pay it up-to-date" and offered $500 a week for information on the California tracks. "I was giving them some of my morning line, late jockey changes, track conditions, anything they would ask." Despite Chicago Crime Commission director Virgil Peterson's claim that when Jack Dragna's "payout" ended he came to Chicago to get "back on the payroll or else," Peterson could not furnish evidence to substantiate the allegation or even prove Dragna visited Chicago during that timeframe. When asked if this was true, Dragna replied, "I don't remember." His attorney Samuel Kurland then explained the LAPD took "all of the records, papers, checks, bills, notes, correspondence," and so on, "from his house, without right or pretense of right, on the night of February 13, 1950." (Niotta Collection.)

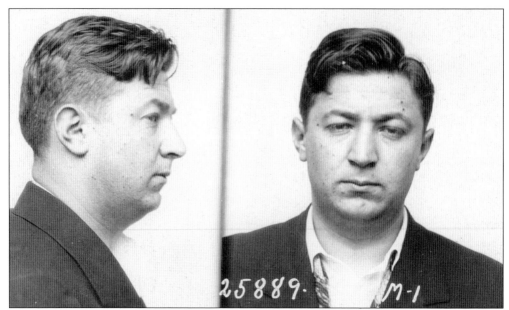

Edward Margolis (above) hit newspapers out west following a 1927 rumrunning arrest involving a police shootout along the Laguna Beach coast. After Prohibition, Margolis shifted into the lucrative bookmaking racket, and in 1948, he acquired the Las Vegas Santa Anita Turf Club (below, formerly McAfee's Mandalay Bar), partnering with the Stearns brothers, Dave and Sam. Wanting to offer patrons offtrack betting, Dave Stearns reached out to former Bugsy Siegel partner Moe Sedway. The pair had Siegel in common. Stearns and Siegel both owned a piece of the Northern Club. Knowing Sedway managed the Golden Nugget Racing Service—the Las Vegas monopoly on the wire as Continental's distributor—Margolis and the Stearns pleaded. Because it would infringe heavily upon the East Coast syndicate's action at the Frontier Club, their request was denied. The establishments, addressed at 113 and 117 Fremont Street, were physically connected. (Both, Bash Collection.)

Furious, Dave Stearns threatened Sedway (above left with entertainer Eddie Cantor) and then offered Dragna and Roselli in Los Angeles a cut if they could obtain the wire. Dragna visited Sedway's partner, Eastern syndicate representative Morris Rosen. Rosen took control of the Flamingo with Sedway after Siegel's assassination. His son Jack also married Siegel's daughter Millicent. When Dragna dismissed his complaint that "a new race wire service would ruin the Frontier," Rosen contacted Eastern leaders Meyer Lansky and Frank Costello. Lansky approached New York boss Tommy Lucchese for assistance. Being a close friend of Dragna, Lucchese was no help. When the Santa Anita finally opened, it did offer patrons offtrack betting—though they provided this service by pirating the competition. A loudspeaker broadcasted the race results that were picked up by a microphone hidden in the El Dorado's ceiling. The setup ended when a passing taxi picked up the signal on a shortwave radio. When arrested for illegally broadcasting race results, the trio countered by suing Continental, Sedway, and Rosen for conducting a monopoly. The suit essentially sanctioned the Race Wire Service Law, breaking the monopoly. (Bash Collection.)

Although Mickey Cohen's autobiography speculated that Jack Dragna and Tommy Lucchese were cousins, the pair were merely close friends and business associates who met back in New York prior to Prohibition. Jack's nephew Louie Tom Dragna (far left) and the syndicate's fight promoter, New York's Lucchese crime family member Frankie Carbo, are pictured in handcuffs after a day in court in 1961. They faced charges for attempting to muscle in on the boxing contract of welterweight champion Don Jordan. (Niotta Collection.)

Jordan, pictured below in 1959 with pal and former boxer Mickey Cohen, won the welterweight title at Los Angeles's Olympic Auditorium in 1958. Following Jordan's second victory, Carbo approached boxing manager Jackie Leonard and asked for a sizeable ongoing cut of the fighter's future earnings. (Niotta Collection.)

Seeking guidance, Leonard telephoned International Boxing Club president Truman Gibson (right) in Chicago. In league with Carbo and Philly fight promotor Frank "Blinky" Palermo, Gibson advised, "Just go along with Carbo and he'll make you a millionaire." When Leonard refused, threats from Joe Sica and Palermo began. Leonard was even hospitalized with a concussion. Taking a beating, Leonard relayed Carbo's threats to the California State Athletic Commission. "He'd have my eyeballs torn out if I talked," Leonard divulged, saying Palermo stated, "We're in for half of the fighter." An indictment followed. Fight promoter Don Fraser commented, "Carbo, Palermo, Sica—they were so menacing-looking. You could tell just by looking at them that they didn't get where they were by looking like a banker." Below, Palermo (in black) sits between comedy duo Abbot and Costello, promoting a 1949 Lou Costello Foundation benefit fight. (Right, Niotta Collection; below, Bash Collection.)

LIST OF EXCLUDED PERSONS

STATE GAMING CONTROL BOARD

NAME/ALIASES							
LOUIS TOM DRAGNA							

SEX	RACE	HT	WT	HAIR	EYES	BUILD	OTHER CHARACTERISTICS
M	W	72	180	Gry	Brn	Medium	

DATE OF BIRTH	PLACE OF BIRTH	FBI	CII
July 18, 1920	California	4 677 209	337 487

LAST KNOWN ADDRESS
21546 Covina Hills Road, Covina, California

DATE LAST UPDATE	OTHER INFO
Jan. 23, 1975	Business Address: Roberta Manufacturing co, Inc. 3330 N. San Gabriel, Rosemead, Cal.

PLACED ON LIST	COMMISSION'S FINAL DECISION	PHOTO DATE
June 13, 1960	June 13, 1960	Feb. 6, 1960

When Blinky Palermo first entered Jackie Leonard's office, he was accompanied by Louie Tom Dragna. Leonard explained that Louie said little, was polite, and this was their only interaction. Despite this, Louie received a five-year-sentence. In 1960, he was also included in the newly created Nevada Black Book. His name sat among the first dozen inductees blacklisted from gaming establishments statewide. Carbo received 25 years but saw early release in 1975. He died that following year. Blinky's parole came in the early 1970s. In 2014, the Nevada Gaming Control Board finally removed deceased one-time acting boss Louie Tom Dragna from the List of Excluded Persons. He passed at age 92 on November 16, 2012. The commission eventually took Joe Sica from the book in 1998. He had been dead for more than five years. (Both, Bash Collection.)

Opened in 1946 by Milton Berle, the Friars Club of Beverly Hills was a well-respected organization that hosted celebrity roasts and benefits, raising millions of dollars for charity. But behind the windowless facade of the Santa Monica building was a locked room accessible only to key-carrying-members. There, Hollywood's elite held high-stakes gin rummy games with winnings reaching $100,000. In June 1962, longstanding member Maurice Friedman, a wealthy Las Vegas developer and habitual card cheat, developed a successful method for winning. After paying the club manager to access the building during off-hours, Friedman had an associate install camouflaged peek holes in the ceiling above gaming tables, where a hidden partner could view opponents' cards and transmit coded signals to a cheating player via shortwave radio. As the scam generated exorbitant profits, the team added more partners. But when newly sponsored friar Johnny Roselli grew wise, he insisted on a one-fifth partnership. Roselli's membership was sponsored by celebrity singer and Friars Club abbot Frank Sinatra. Sinatra is pictured above right, presenting a Friars Club award to entertainer Jack Benny. (Niotta Collection.)

Roselli's role in the partnership proved more advisory. Victims claimed they rarely saw him participating in games but rather observing and monitoring the cards (much like the ones pictured above) to ensure smooth operations. The swindle continued until the summer of 1967, when friar and Las Vegas casino owner Beldon Katleman tipped off a federal agent about the events transpiring at the club. Gaining testimony from one of the partners, the FBI raided, confiscated evidence, and shut down the card games. Authorities estimated the total take may have topped $1 million. One of the victims hit exceedingly hard was millionaire shoe mogul Harry Karl, seen below with his one-time wife, former Bugsy Siegel conquest Marie McDonald. At the trial that followed, the partners received varying penalties. Roselli faced a $55,000 fine and five years of imprisonment. (Above, Niotta Collection; below, Bash Collection.)

Seven

GANG WARFARE AND MURDER

In a nationally broadcasted 1957 television interview with Mike Douglas, Mickey Cohen shockingly confessed, "I have killed no men, that, in the first place didn't deserve killing." Whether factual or an exaggeration, Mickey's infamous quote offers a peek into the gangster mindset and its warped justification for killing those they considered deserving. Perhaps it is this logic that fueled the rampant bloodshed associated with the history of organized crime in Los Angeles. For the continued success of every criminal syndicate, violence, or the threat thereof, proved to be a necessary evil. Often used to instill fear, settle disputes, silence a witness, or claim power, the natural partnership between organized crime and violence has always gone hand in hand. The vicious mobsters applying these tactics understood that enforcing muscle was often the fastest and most straightforward means to an end. In Los Angeles, gangsters employed nearly every method imaginable. In one instance, gambler Les Bruneman was shot in public in broad daylight for bootlegging the racing wire. In another, New York's notorious Murder, Inc., dispatched killers to Los Angeles to silence potential snitch Harry Greenberg. These killings, like many others, proved successful in obtaining the desired goal, maximizing profits, and eliminating outside threats. But not all violence was as calculated. Amid heated arguments, individuals sometimes acted on instinct, as seen in the murder of bodyguard Johnny Stompanato by 14-year-old Cheryl Crane. This was also the case in the slaying of bookie Jack Whalen, who took a bullet in the skull in the middle of a crowded nightclub. Of perhaps the most notoriety among organized crime warfare in Los Angeles is "the Battle of the Sunset Strip." Ben Siegel's assassination spurred a power vacuum that sparked a dispute between the local mafia and the gang led by Mickey Cohen. Bombings and shootings soon became commonplace, with both gangsters and innocent bystanders becoming the unfortunate victims of reckless violence. These all-out gang wars held openly in the streets of Los Angeles set the stage for the city to be dubbed the "gang capital" of the nation in the decades that followed.

On May 20, 1931, bullets claimed the lives of two during a meeting held in the Sunset Boulevard real estate office of Charlie Crawford. Well-timed, the killer struck during the break of Crawford's bodyguard-brother. Hearing shots, George Crawford (left) ran back and found Herbert Spencer dead. His brother Charlie was about to follow. Refusing to name his killer to investigating officers, Crawford mouthed, "If I die, the secret goes with me." Authorities suspected Crawford's former criminal associate Guy McAfee. (Niotta Collection.)

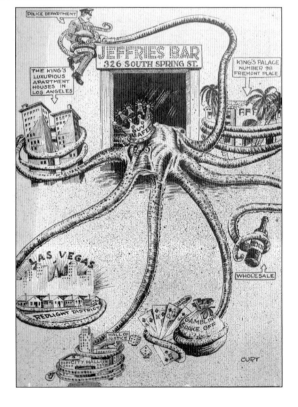

Supplying sufficient motive, victim Herbert Spencer—managing editor at the Crawford-funded *Critic of Critics* magazine—had been smearing McAfee in print, dubbing him "the Capone of the Coast." But the former vice cop's alibi checked out, and three days later, an unlikely confession surfaced—from Los Angeles deputy district attorney and candidate for municipal bench Dave Clark. (*Los Angeles Times* Photographic Archives, b3699_G1062.)

"Debonair Dave" Clark, pictured with his wife and lawyer outside the courthouse, swore he visited Crawford to ask for campaign funds. When "Good Time" Charlie reached for a pistol during heated political debate, however, Clark proved quicker. Claiming self-defense, Clark eventually saw acquittal, yet some refused to believe he committed the crime. Herbert Spencer's son Jack told newsmen, "It was someone from the underworld." (Niotta Collection.)

When prosecutor Joe Ford (inspecting Crawford's pistols) put Clark under a lens, his daily planner came in handy. Eight days before the slaying, Clark kept a noon appointment with Jack Dragna. That following day, he met with Sam Bruno and then Tom Dragna. Bruno's name appeared again on May 15 and 16, just days before the crime. Testimony uncovered that Clark had recently racked up a large debt at Agua Caliente. Nervous, he purchased a pistol. (Niotta Collection.)

As an added twist, the detectives who questioned Charlie Crawford just before he passed swore the victim admitted that two men barged in and started shooting. Police department ballistics experts captain Edward Crossman and Spencer Moxley (above) both testified that they were unable to determine whether the bullets that killed Herbert Spencer and Charlie Crawford came from the same weapon. Two pistols could have been used. Word of a retrial was dropped after Crawford's widow expressed a lack of confidence in a conviction. Following the scandal that smashed Dave Clark's political and legal career, he came to work for Guy McAfee exclusively. But even gainfully employed, matters did not end well for Debonair Dave. After his wife left him, he took to the bottle heavily, succumbing to depression. When a former law partner and friend let him stay at his home in 1953, Dave thanked his host by taking a 12-gauge shotgun to the lawyer's wife. Three weeks into a five-to-life sentence, a brain hemorrhage finally ended Debonair Dave's suffering. (Niotta Collection.)

Although crime scenes could be gruesome, some victims simply vanished. In 1934, the Los Angeles courts finally declared the deaths of four long missing under questionable circumstances. In May 1929, Joe Porazzo's bullet-ridden sedan turned up. Porazzo was never found. Six months later, vineyardist Frank Baumgarteker disappeared after telling Ardizzone and Dragna he no longer wanted his land used for bootlegging endeavors. Falling out with the brugad, Tony Buccola lost his Los Angeles privileges. Although allowed to return when his mother fell ill, Tony vanished in May 1930, shortly after her passing. He was last seen dining with Ardizzone, Frank Borgia, and Big George Niotta. Joe Ardizzone disappeared after leaving his ranch October 15, 1931. His brother Frank told investigators, "Don't bother looking for any enemies. It'll be one of his friends." In 1968, an agent referenced Nicola Gentile's manuscript and suggested their informant be questioned to "determine if he knew whether Ardizzone's death came about as part of the purge of Maranzano's sympathizers," during the Castellammarese War. Above, district attorney Buron Fitts (left) confers with ex-convict Leonard Wolfe about the possible whereabouts of Frank Baumgarteker's body. (Niotta Collection.)

Although gambler Les Bruneman (above left with attorney Jerry Giesler) survived an attack in July 1937, he was not so lucky on October 25. When two gunmen entered the Roost Café at 2700 West Temple Street and spotted their target, they delivered 11 slugs. In an attempt to tackle a gunman, café employee Frank Greuzard (left) was also murdered. In *The Green Felt Jungle* (1963), Ovid Demaris and Ed Reid blamed Bugsy for the hit, fabricating a scene where the mobster called the city's bookmakers together then demanded a tariff. Bruneman "was the only hood to stand up and voice objection" and paid for it. Demaris later contradicted himself in *The Last Mafioso* (1980). Faulting the racing wire, he stated Bruneman bootlegged Johnny Roselli's service, and after they "got into a beef," Dragna "gave Bomp the contract." The second version rings a little closer to the truth. (Both, Bash Collection.)

Bruneman's murder spurred eight subpoenas—Los Angeles gambling barons McAfee, Scherer, two Page brothers, Nealis, Chuck Addison, Dragna, and Roselli. Neither the press nor the district attorney's office mentioned Benjamin Siegel. Although the local brugad was responsible, sadly, someone else took the fall. Mistakenly identified by a witness, Pete Pianezzi received life and served 13 years. Pianezzi is pictured with his lawyer, who asked in vain, "Can you say this is the man?" (Niotta Collection.)

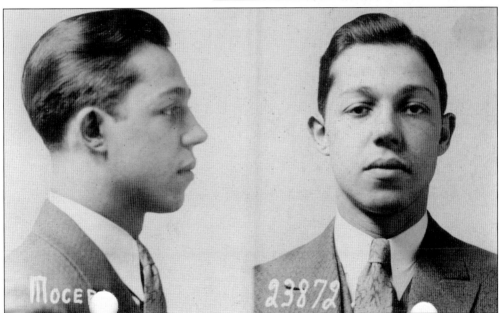

Pianezzi sat in prison until being paroled in 1953. Although Gov. Pat Brown pardoned him in 1966, Pianezzi's name was not officially cleared with a full pardon until 1981. The decision was sparked by the revealing confession of government witness Jimmy the Weasel Fratianno. The true killers, Leo "Lips" Moceri (above) and Frank "the Bomp" Bompensiero, were already dead. (Bash Collection.)

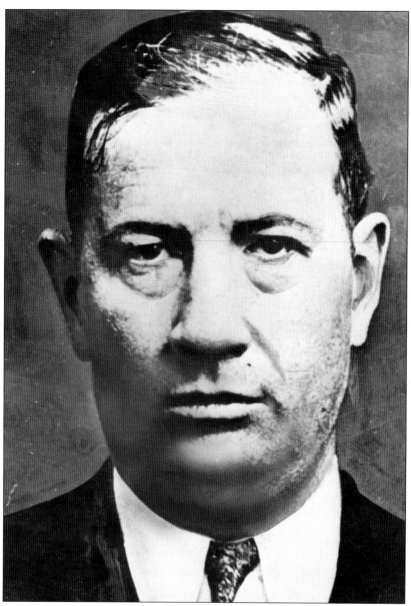

Harry "Big Greenie" Greenberg, also known as Harry Schachter, was a New York mobster who grew up on the streets of Brooklyn alongside future Murder, Inc., associates Louis "Lepke" Buchalter and Bugsy Siegel. As Murder, Inc., began unraveling in the late 1930s, associates told Greenberg to go on the lam, keep quiet, and stay out of trouble. While hiding out in Canada, Greenberg sent a vague threat to Murder, Inc., boss Lepke Buchalter, requesting $5,000 to remain silent. Realizing the error in his financial request, Greenberg fled to Detroit and then Los Angeles. When word got out that Greenberg was hiding in his newly adopted hometown, Siegel insisted on handling the hit personally and assembled a team that included Albert "Tic Toc" Tannenbaum and Frankie "The Wop" Carbo. On the night of November 22, 1939, Siegel and his team waited outside Greenberg's Hollywood Hills home. When his car parked, Frankie Carbo sprang into action, blasting five shots into Greenberg's head. Behind the wheel of the stolen getaway car sat Bugsy Siegel. (Bash Collection.)

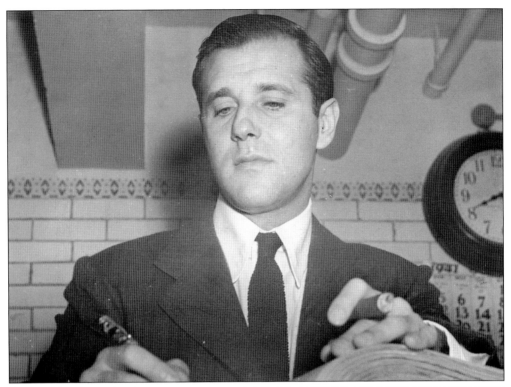

Authorities investigating the Greenberg murder were unable to tie any individuals to the crime until the Spring of 1940, when Murder, Inc., member Abe "Kid Twist" Reles turned informant and began to sing. After being named as a participant in the hit, Tannenbaum flipped as well and laid out all the first-hand details of the crime. On August 20, 1940, a grand jury issued indictments charging Siegel, Carbo, Buchalter, and two others with murder. Siegel was arrested in Los Angeles and booked in the county jail (above). Unable to locate Carbo, the LAPD issued wanted posters for his arrest (right). That following summer, he

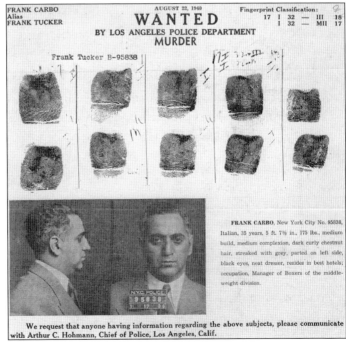

FRANK CARBO
Alias
FRANK TUCKER

AUGUST 22, 1940

WANTED
BY LOS ANGELES POLICE DEPARTMENT
MURDER

Frank Tucker B-95838

Fingerprint Classification:
17 I 32 — III 18
I 32 — MII 17

FRANK CARBO, New York City No. 95838, Italian, 35 years, 5 ft. 7½ in., 175 lbs., medium build, medium complexion, dark curly chestnut hair, streaked with grey, parted on left side, black eyes, neat dresser, resides in best hotels; occupation, Manager of Boxers of the middle-weight division.

We request that anyone having information regarding the above subjects, please communicate with Arthur C. Hohmann, Chief of Police, Los Angeles, Calif.

finally surrendered. After multiple dismissals and retrials, the case ultimately died along with its star witness. While in police custody, Reles mysteriously fell to his death from the window of his Coney Island hotel room. (Both, Bash Collection.)

Benjamin "Bugsy" Siegel's move to Southern California during the second half of the 1930s has given rise to tales of East Coast operators desperate to set up shop out west. Some stories have even erroneously spouted that Los Angeles was an "open country." Dramatic as the plot sounds, this went against the very premise of the New York Commission—a governing body formed to avoid encroachment and war. In *The Last Testament of Bill Bonanno*, the New York Cosa Nostra member and son of boss Joe Bonanno clarified that "it wasn't the Commission who sent Bugsy Siegel to California," as the commission "did not have the authority to make that decision." An equal amount of—if not more—mystery and myth surrounds Siegel's relationship with the local brugad and his infamous and still unsolved murder. More than a few theories have surfaced in the seven some decades since shots fired through the window of the rented Beverly Hills mansion on 810 North Linden Lane. (Bash Collection.)

On June 20, 1947, Siegel picked up a complimentary newspaper from Jack's at the Beach after dining with friends. He was reading on the sofa when nine .30-caliber slugs tore into his body. Detectives noted the front page of the newspaper resting on his lap had been stamped "GOOD NIGHT, SLEEP WELL WITH THE COMPLIMENTS OF JACK'S," offering irony for those believing Jack Dragna was responsible. Other theories blame the Flamingo Hotel and Casino, from which Siegel was allegedly skimming, and a dispute over control of the racing wire. The LAPD advised feds that two months earlier, Jack Dragna and Mickey Cohen met in Los Angeles with Chicago Outfit representatives Jake "Greasy Thumbs" Guzik and Murray "the Camel" Humphreys to discuss Siegel's fate. Perhaps equally puzzling to mob aficionados is the whodunit aspect of the crime. (Above, Bash Collection; below, Niotta Collection.)

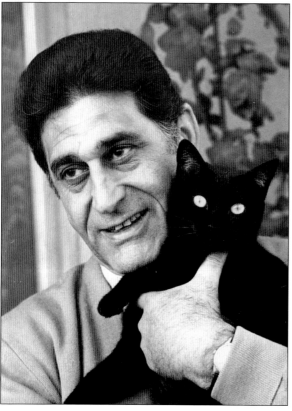

Was it Frankie Carbo on Lansky's orders from New York or ex-war hero Bob McDonald paying off debts to Jack Dragna? Was it Moose Padza aiding his mistress, Bea Sedway, the wife of Siegel's business partner Moe Sedway, or did the Marine brother of Siegel's girlfriend, Virginia Hill, strike to end the abuse of his sister? Though the truth may never surface, at least one suspect offered his story. In 1987, shortly before his death, former Dragna gopher Eddie Cannizzaro (left) took the credit. The Cat Man of Agoura Hills, as his neighbors called him, explained that Siegel's childhood friend and business partner, Meyer Lansky (above, far left with lawyers), plotted with associate Joe Adonis. Because Siegel resided in Jack Dragna's territory, the local brugad was given the contract, and Cannizzaro claimed that he fulfilled it. (Above, Bash Collection; below, Niotta Collection.)

Victim of Ambush

On February 28, 1950, police failed to protect their star witness, allowing an assassin to deliver a .32 caliber slug into the temple of 28-year-old Abraham Davidian (right) while he slept on the sofa in his mother's Fresno residence. Scheduled to testify in a case against over a dozen indicted on narcotics charges, the killing left authorities empty-handed. The 1978 crime commission's Historical Perspective explains, "Mickey Cohen was sent to the West Coast by Eastern syndicate leaders" and proved "instrumental in setting up narcotic operations through Mexico and California" with "Joseph and Alfred Sica." Just before Christmas of 1950, brothers Joe and Fred Sica (below) received an early present. Although implicated by "Singing Abe" as his heroin supplier and tabbed by the crime commission as "overlords of the multi-million-dollar dope traffic," Davidian's murder freed the pair of all charges. (Right, Niotta Collection; below, Bash Collection.)

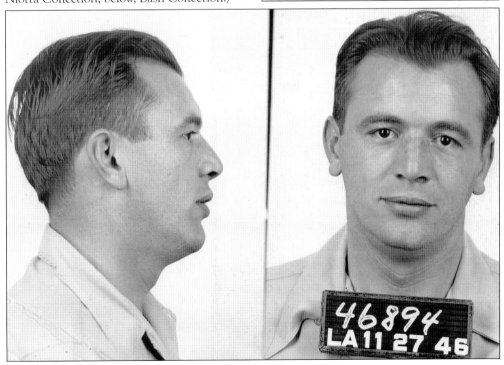

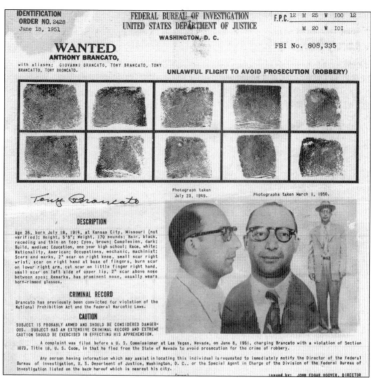

Kansas City hoodlums Anthony Brancato and Anthony Trombino, known as the Two Tonys, were muscle-men and shakedown artists who made their living preying on bookies and gamblers. Wild-eyed and reckless, the team paid little mind to who they ripped off. In June 1951, the pair netted $35,000 after robbing the bookmaking office of the Las Vegas Flamingo Hotel. Identified during the robbery, the duo was arrested but skipped town after arranging bail. The FBI issued a warrant for "unlawful flight to avoid prosecution (above)." Continuing their shakedown tactics in Los Angeles, the two collected $3,000 from bookie Sam Lazes. But when they pocketed the cash, their employer contacted Jack Dragna. Deciding the two were no good and had to go, Dragna gave the assignment to Jimmy Fratianno, who arranged a meeting with the Two Tonys at the apartment of his friend Sam London (below). (Both, Bash Collection.)

During their August 6, 1951, meeting, Fratianno learned that the Two Tonys had been shaking down mob-protected bookies to cover legal expenses from the Flamingo arrest. Hearing this, Fratianno baited them with an opportunity to rob a high-stakes poker game later that night. To establish an alibi, he went over the plan with his hit-team at Nick Licata's Five O'Clock Club. Fratianno and Charles "Batts" Battaglia (above) were designated shooters and Leo "Lips" Moceri and Angelo Polizzi the getaway drivers. Fratianno and Charlie Batts arrived outside London's apartment around 9:00 p.m. After sliding into the backseat of Trombino's car, Fratianno fired twice into 36-year-old Brancato's head. Seeing Batts frozen, he delivered five rounds into 31-year-old Trombino. Police questioned nearly 60 suspects and held 14, but the case fell apart when a waitress at Licata's club corroborated their whereabouts. (Above, Bash Collection; below, Niotta Collection.)

After settling in Los Angeles, former US Marine Johnny Stompanato caught the eye of gangster Mickey Cohen and soon made the dangerous decision to become Mickey's bodyguard and enforcer. Shootouts had already claimed the lives of two previous candidates. Enjoying the Hollywood nightlife and his minor celebrity status, Stompanato acclimated to the life, and in 1957, he began dating movie star Lana Turner. The pair are seen together at a Hollywood masquerade party. Their love affair grew tumultuous, and soon, lavish gifts and love notes turned into arguments and physical abuse. The couple shared their final heated confrontation on the night of April 4, 1958. When Turner's daughter, Cheryl, overheard yelling from the bedroom of their Beverly Hills home, she knew violence was imminent. And once threats of physical abuse were shouted, the 14-year-old girl ran to the kitchen and grabbed a carving knife. As Stompanato and Turner left the bedroom in shouts, a panicked Cheryl plunged the knife deep into Stompanato's stomach. Stunned, he gasped his last breath. (Bash Collection.)

The stabbing of gangster Stompanato by a movie star's child caused a media frenzy across the nation. A week after the slaying, an inquest was held to determine how Stompanato died and who, if anyone, was criminally responsible. Called to testify were Mickey Cohen, who refused to talk; Cheryl's father, actor Stephen Crane; the detectives who arrived at the scene; and Lana Turner (right), whose testimony many considered among her most exceptional performances. (Bash Collection.)

The jury deemed the stabbing a justifiable homicide, and although absolved of any wrongdoing, the incident remained a stain on the career and reputation of both Lana and her daughter. As for Stompanato, his body was returned to his hometown of Woodstock, Illinois. There he received a military funeral (left) attended by relatives and friends before being laid to rest in his family's Oakland Cemetery plot. (Bash Collection.)

During Prohibition, career criminal Fred Whalen ran liquor into California. In hopes of a better life for his son Jack, he shipped the 11-year-old boy off to Hollywood to attend a prestigious military school. After some minor run-ins with the law as a teenager, Jack Whalen joined the Air Force, and in 1943 he married Kay Sabichi. The debutante's family was among Los Angeles's oldest and wealthiest. Resettling back in Hollywood with dreams of becoming a movie star, Whalen took on the stage name Jack O'Hara. He even commissioned a group of studio photographs showcasing his different looks. But with minor film roles far and few between, Whalen continually found himself looking for action and resorting to crime in order to provide for his wife and young daughter. Racking up a series of arrests for assault, extortion, and bookmaking, full-time criminal Jack Whalen became widely known as "The Enforcer." The independent tough handled muscle jobs for the syndicate and the Italians and, eventually, gained the reputation as the bookmaking king of the San Fernando Valley. (Bash Collection.)

Looking to collect a $390 gambling debt and settle a beef with a couple of Mickey Cohen's associates, Whalen went to Rondelli's restaurant in Sherman Oaks on the night of December 3, 1959. He found the two he was after, Sam La Cigno (bottom left) and George Piscitelle, sitting at Mickey's booth with two others. Approaching the group, Whalen demanded the pair settle their debts. When an argument erupted, Whalen delivered a sharp right to Piscitelle and then turned his attention to La Cigno. But before the next punch flew, the gangster opened fire. A .38 round hit Whalen right between the eyes. When the police arrived, Whalen was dead and La Cigno was nowhere to be found. A week later, the shooter finally surrendered, claiming he acted in self-defense. (Both, Bash Collection.)

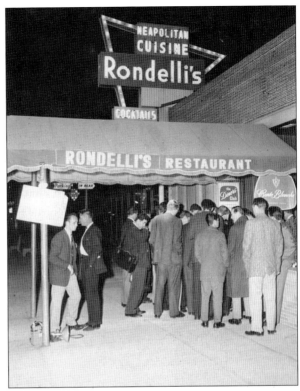

After Benjamin Siegel's murder, Mickey Cohen tried taking over the gangster's rackets but soon faced opposition from Los Angeles boss Jack Dragna. Although Mickey dubbed it "a battle of recognition," alleging that Dragna's pride was hurt, Jimmy Fratianno revealed monetary motivation. With Mickey gone, the brugad could partner with Undersheriff Al Guasti in collecting $80,000 a week in protection from vendors in Mickey's territory. The chaos started when Simone Scozzari, Frank Bompensiero, Sam Bruno, Biaggio Bonventre, and Frank DeSimone shot up Mickey's Sunset Strip haberdashery on August 18, 1948. A round nicked Jimmie Rist in the cheek, doctors feared Albert "Slick" Snyder might lose his arm, and Mickey's lieutenant—45-year-old Harry "Hooky" Rothman (above)—wound up with a bullet in his head. Mickey's neurotic habit of frequent handwashing (left) served as a blessing. He was in the restroom when the excitement began. (Both, Bash Collection.)

Arrested with his crew in March 1949 after beating shopkeeper Alfred Pearson, Mickey posted a $100,000 bond, using his house as collateral, to spring Frank Niccoli (right) and Dave Ogul. Mysteriously, the pair went missing shortly after. Although police learned that Niccoli dined with Fratianno just before his disappearance, ultimately authorities believed Mickey's men had merely skipped town. Later, Fratianno divulged he strangled Niccoli to hit Mickey financially. When the pair failed to appear, Mickey forfeited their $75,000 bail. Unlike Niccoli, Ogul's fate was tied to a fellow henchman—narcotics figure Harold "Happy" Meltzer (below). When New York put a murder contract on Happy's head for talking to law enforcement, Happy ran to the Dragnas. Federal files indicate he agreed to "deliver OGUL to DRAGNA to square himself," and "through some ruse, trapped him and clubbed him to death." (Both, Bash Collection.)

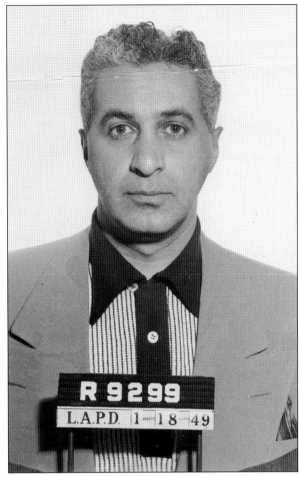

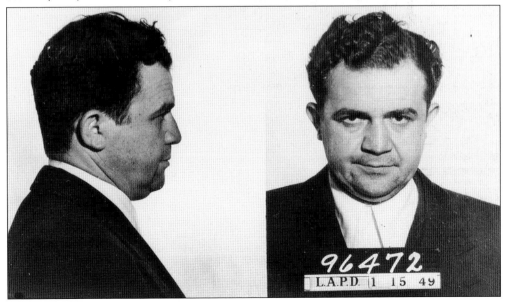

By now, Mickey Cohen's crew had begun threatening bookies and muscling the Los Angeles race books. Mickey still called the hat shop on Sunset headquarters. Although he fortified the establishment, installing bulletproof doors and burglar alarms, the upgrades failed to deter the local brugad. In June, gangster squad head Lt. William Burns divulged two newer attempts on Mickey's life. Detectives were investigating a dynamite bundle with a half-burned fuse discovered beneath the gambler's Brentwood home and had learned that his bullet-peppered sedan was sitting in a repair shop with its interior stained in blood. The brugad struck just as Mickey pulled into his driveway. "I fell to the floor," Mickey expressed, "and drove that goddamn car from San Vicente Boulevard all the ways down to Wilshire with one hand." Shards of glass littered his face, staining the interior. After the incident, Mickey spent $17,000 armoring a Cadillac with bulletproof tires and windows. But when denied a permit to operate his new tank, he sold at a loss for $12,000. Today, the vehicle resides at New Zealand's Southward Car Museum. (Courtesy of Southward Car Museum.)

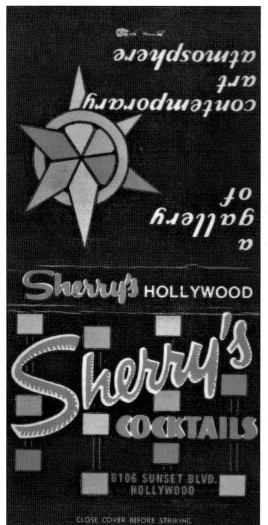

When Mickey and his entourage spilled out into the parking lot of Sherry's on Sunset Boulevard (above left) at 3:45 a.m. on July 20, 1949, rifle and shotgun blasts welcomed his party, claiming collateral damage. Injured by ricochet was 26-year-old bit actress Dee Davis (above right), who received four wounds in her back. Shooters also tagged journalist Florabel Muir in the rear. Initial reports dubbed the hit an amateur job, but after closer study, detectives noted assailants had carefully planned a well-timed plot. Ordinarily, Mickey's men adhered to a strict routine whenever they left Sherry's. Conducting plenty of surveillance, the brugad learned these moves. However, on the day of the attempted hit, Mickey's driver got lazy and abandoned protocol. The careless action saved Mickey by placing a Cadillac in front of the line of fire. (Both, Niotta Collection.)

When a 30.06 round zipped clean through his arm, Mickey felt so dazed he just stood there worrying about his suit. Meanwhile, agent Harry Cooper—a 38-year-old bodyguard assigned to Cohen by California attorney general Fred Howser—took a slug to the liver. But Hooky's replacement, Edward "Neddie" Herbert, tasted the worst of the attack, wounded in the spleen and kidney. By the time they sped for the hospital, he was already in shock. The New York office of the FBI listed Neddie "as an ex-killer for BENJAMIN 'BUGS' SIEGEL." Mickey called him "one of my strong right arms." In a wiretap conversation recorded in November 1947, Neddie told Mickey, "I'm getting out of this. I want to live to be a grandfather." Instead he slipped into a coma on July 26, 1949, and died two days later. (Both, Bash Collection.)

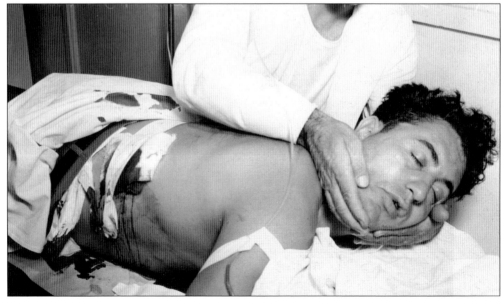

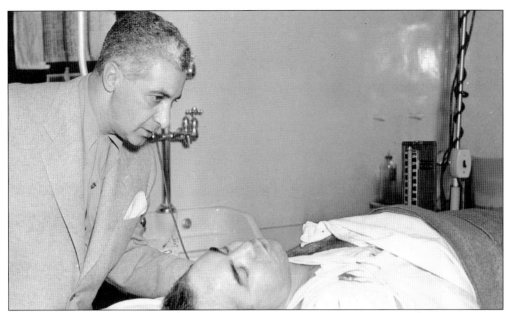

Although investigators questioned Jack Dragna, they were not sure who put Mickey in the hospital (in bed with Niccoli standing above him). Intelligence suggested Eastern mobsters. Highlighting the still fresh Brenda Allen scandal, Frank Tremaine's column offered the following insight from the underworld: "Cohen was blasted because he opened up this town so nobody could make two bits" and "any one of a thousand guys could have been after Mickey." Proving this point, military veterans formed a vigilante group to get rid of Mickey that August. Wrongly, Mickey felt Dragna associate Jimmy Utley (below, wearing hat, booked for extortion in 1939) was responsible. Right around the time of Mickey's death, Fratianno revealed the shooters' identities to special agent Larry Lawrence. He named a little known player called "Army" and Mickey's former pal. Like Happy, Jimmy Regace had joined the Italians. (Above, Bash Collection; below; Niotta Collection.)

Although a bomb detonated beneath Mickey Cohen's Brentwood home on February 6, 1950, luck saved the gambler's life yet again. A floor safe deflected the blast. Mickey is depicted assessing damage to his tailored suits (left) and confronting detectives (right). Following the Valentine's Day release of Gov. Earl Warren's crime commission report, which accused 55-year-old banana merchant Jack Dragna of being Los Angeles's mafia boss, the LAPD hauled in the Dragnas for questioning. The 69-page document identified Jack as Mickey's main competition in Los Angeles's bookmaking rackets and even commented on their fight—"Cohen has backed down," has "no appetite for a struggle with his rival," and "seven members of Cohen's gang deserted last year to Dragna." Responding to the press, Mickey lied, saying Dragna "is one of my closest friends and not a rival of any kind." (Left, Bash Collection; right, Niotta Collection.)

Charging conspiracy to commit murder, the LAPD rounded up Dragna's nephew Louie, his brother Tom, Frank Paul, underboss Momo Adamo, and nephew (also) Frank Paul (above). Officers also confiscated an arsenal (right); however, Jack later testified the intelligence division planted these weapons. Unable to locate Jack, a manhunt commenced. Newsmen printed rumors that he fled to Nicaragua on his *Santa Maria* banana boat. To the shame of the LAPD, when Jack surfaced a few weeks later for an interview on March 9, 1950, he told the *Los Angeles Daily Mirror* that he never left. "A rookie officer cited Dragna on two occasions for traffic violations, once on February 15 and again on February 28." Comically, the wanted man waltzed straight into the police station and paid his fine. Newspapers printed his citation and check. Backpedaling, Chief Worton commented Dragna was no longer a suspect. (Both, Bash Collection.)

On December 11, 1950, a 12-gauge double-barrel Remington ended the life of Mickey's lawyer, "underworld mouthpiece" Samuel Rummel (above). Angelo Polizzi squeezed the trigger, and Nick Licata's son Carlo assisted on the hit. The pair became made mafia members a year later, and Polizzi eventually rose to caporegime. The trend of Mickey's men dying, disappearing, or trading sides was no secret to the press or law enforcement. Each took turns razzing the gambler about his losses. Intelligence division captain Lynn White told reporters that Dragna was Los Angeles's "top dog," and Mickey Cohen "couldn't carry lead pencils for him." Although Hollywood has since glamorized "the little gambler" as some sort of king in Los Angeles, in reality, he and his men never harmed a single member of the Los Angeles Brugad. The Battle of the Sunset Strip ended in the summer of 1951 after taxmen nailed Mickey. Four years of prison awaited. Federal files indicate that his bookmaking rackets and union interests went to Jack Dragna. Mickey sat in prison until a few months before Jack's death. (*Los Angeles Times* Photographic Archives, uclalat_1429_b112_67661-1.)

Eight

FALL OF THE
LOS ANGELES MAFIA

Crime fighters and crime writers have discussed the coastal differences between Los Angeles gangsters and their Eastern counterparts. The smaller West Coast family had difficulties controlling such a vast territory, which spanned from the San Diego, California–Tijuana, Mexico, border all the way up to Santa Barbara and at one-time also included Southern Nevada. Also problematic, as the FBI files state, were the "many overlapping jurisdictions of investigative agencies," which made it "almost impossible to establish any connections with law enforcement which would be of enduring value." This reality made payoffs exceedingly intricate and costly. After greasing one pocket, another hand always seemed ready. For this reason, all-out dominance never had a place in Los Angeles, and the rackets were handled in another manner—through a delicate system of corruption run out of the mayor's office. Members of the district attorney's office, the LAPD, and the sheriff's department were in on the take. This different approach has fueled claims that the western brugad was small-time or "Mickey Mouse," but the derogatory handle of a "Mickey Mouse Mafia" does not appear in any early newspaper article, crime book, or FBI file. The phrase went viral in 1984 after police chief Daryl Gates used it to reference the Los Angeles family's current leadership. This era proved especially turbulent for Angeleno mafiosos, who suffered immense troubles in controlling rackets and staying out of jail. But Los Angeles was not alone. On the same timeline, journalists noted the dwindling strength of the Detroit Partnership and referred to Philly's Bruno-Scarfo family as the ineffective aging Geritol Gang. Although Sen. Estes Kefauver's televised crime hearings of the early 1950s and the infamous mafia summit bust in Apalachin, New York, later that decade, brought the nation's gangsterdom problem out into the open, the primary downfall of La Cosa Nostra countrywide was internal. In fact, the "Mickey Mouse Mafia" title took root in informant activity. In 1980, Chicago newsmen leaked a wiretapped telephone conversation, which "picked up references by Chicago mobsters to the 'Mickey Mouse Mafia' in California." These gangsters were no doubt heated over Jimmy the Weasel Fratianno's recent courtroom tour. He was testifying against his fellow mafiosos.

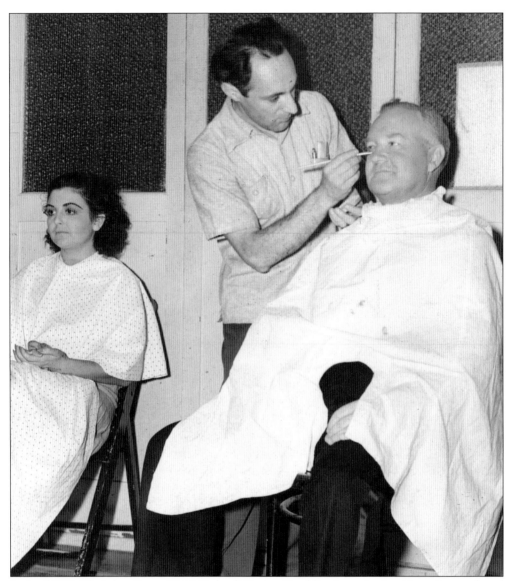

In April 1950, Chairman Ernest W. McFarland's Senate Gambling Investigating Committee gathered in Washington, DC, to discuss eradicating the racing wire service. Although top officials from all over the nation testified before Congress, Los Angeles authorities stole the spotlight. Calling Los Angeles a "lush field" with a "large number of people who like to gamble," Los Angeles Mayor Fletcher Bowron (pictured during makeup before a broadcast television appearance) estimated annual gambling profits reached half a billion. After declaring bookmaking, "the most menacing in the entire field of organized crime," he stated, "horseracing is legal in California," making judges "reluctant to punish bookies." LAPD captain Lynn White and interim police chief Worton, who had just relinquished his temporary position to Chief William H. Parker, explained that "a nationwide crime and gambling syndicate" existed and that James Ragen's assassination clearly illustrated this largescale connection. After Arizona senator McFarland met with Tennessee senator Carey Estes Kefauver that next month, Kefauver—head of the Senate Crime Investigating Committee—alerted the press that he would complete McFarland's work and show "the dissemination of racing news is a gangster monopoly." (Niotta Collection.)

SENATOR

Estes

KEFAUVER

"California's Adopted Son"

THE WINNING DEMOCRAT

FOR

PRESIDENT

Donning presidential aspirations, Kefauver established a committee intent upon showing Americans a nationwide criminal syndicate existed. During a 17-month span, the committee held public hearings in 14 major cities, calling 600 witnesses. Some proceedings were even televised. But Kefauver had help setting the stage. In 1947, California governor Earl Warren formed the Standley Commission, which generated four reports over 32 months of digging. Come 1951, the Hunt Commission emerged, delivering further insight into California crime in 1953. Jack Dragna's testimony in Chicago linked him to Lucky Luciano, Frank Costello, Vito Genovese, Tommy Lucchese, Vincent Mangano, Joe Profaci, and more. He and 32 others were cited for contempt for failing to answer questions. But rather than unravel a mafia plot, Kefauver's efforts revealed the rampant willingness of corrupt officials. These findings were soon overshadowed by the Communist threat and the Korean War. (Both, Niotta Collection.)

On November 14, 1957, Joe "the Barber" Barbara, boss of the Pittston crime family (later renamed the Bufalino family) hosted a mob summit at his Apalachin estate to discuss the recent unsanctioned assassination of boss Albert Anastasia. Los Angeles Brugad leader Frank DeSimone and underboss Simone Scozzari (left) attended the New York meet, along with over 100 other high-ranking members. When authorities grew wise, however, they set up roadblocks then raided. Agents chased fleeing mobsters through the compound and surrounding forest, detaining 62, including Los Angeles's leadership. Most attendees received prison sentences and hefty fines. More importantly, the event proved what Kefauver could not—a nationwide criminal syndicate truly did exist. New members were not made for years following the bust. At his trial, the judge ordered Simone Scozzari deported back to his native Italy. Above, Scozzari is escorted by a detention officer to a waiting Rome-bound flight. (Bash Collection.)

The Apalachin bust solidified New York boss Joe Bonanno's dislike for Los Angeles leader Frank DeSimone. But plotting to kill a boss and take his territory brought consequences. After the commission exiled Bonanno from the mafia, he relocated to Arizona. A decade later, the retired godfather made a second bid. FBI files reveal that "of the estimated 200 Mafiosi who reside in the Los Angeles area, not more than 70 show loyalty to Nicolo Licata." Capitalizing on this dissension, Bonanno hoped to implant his son, Cosa Nostra member Bill Bonanno, as Los Angeles's new boss. Pictured, Joe is seated to the left of young Bill (center), directly across from his cousin and Buffalo boss Stefano Magaddino. Seeking local help in a coup, Joe Bonanno enticed disgruntled Los Angeles family hitman Frank Bompensiero. The new regime bumped him down to soldier and gave his former position of San Diego caporegime to Tony Mirabile. Vocal about his displeasure, Bompensiero made a perfect candidate. Bonanno also propositioned another Los Angeles member who despised DeSimone—Charlie Batts, who was serving time at Leavenworth. But to their dismay, the commission again refused. (Bash Collection.)

In the 1960s, the feds approached Johnny Roselli about a delicate matter. Agents cornered him while walking in Beverly Hills near Brighton Way and Rodeo Drive. After explaining that they knew his true identity of Filippo Sacco, they waved a copy of his birth certificate and threatened deportation, pointing out that he was not a citizen. Agents even brought a picture of him as a boy with his mother in Boston. Refusing to listen, Roselli simply muttered, "Go see my attorney." Although deportation efforts began, Roselli remained stateside long enough to be assassinated. He did, however, learn who tipped federal agents off—Neapolitan Salvatore "Dago Louie" Piscopo, also known as Louis Merli. Although it came as a surprise, since Roselli and Dago Louie (above) were close for years, the betrayal did not phase Jimmy Fratianno. He and Dago Louie were made during the same ceremony in 1947, and allegedly, Jack Dragna relayed his suspicions to Fratianno years back. Hit by the taxman, Dago Louie started feeding intel to the feds in 1963. He died of natural causes in 1977. (Niotta Collection.)

Getting out of prison in 1960 and being demoted from caporegime to soldier, Frank Bompensiero tried transferring to Chicago with Fratianno and Roselli. Unsuccessful, he became critical of leadership. Federal files indicate he stated, "The boss, FRANK DESIMONE and the underboss, NICK LICATA, were afraid to do anything," and the brugad had "very little going." Federal files also reveal that when Licata took over, "BOMPENSIERO told ROSELLI that he definitely did not care to lend his support." Roselli suggested viewing Licata as an interim boss, but Bomp's behavior grew worse, and he eventually became an informant. Having suspicions, boss Dominic Brooklier decided to have him killed. But knowing Bomp had been a hitman for half a century, Brooklier proceeded cautiously. Putting together a ruse to gain his trust, Tommy Palermo stepped down as consigliere, allowing Bompensiero's promotion. A trap was then set. Bomp was shot in the head in an alley on February 10, 1977, while walking back to his Pacific Beach apartment. He had just finished a telephone call at a nearby phonebooth where the brugad knew he took business calls. (Bash Collection.)

Sixteen months after entering prison for extortion in 1975, the release of boss Dominic Brooklier and underboss Sam Sciortino came in, ending Jimmy Fratianno's (left) run as acting underboss. Although previously a captain, he was reduced from underboss to soldier. Worse still, although they shared a long history, Fratianno now worried Brooklier wanted him dead. Previous boss Nick Licata issued a similar threat years earlier. An informant advised, "Word has been put out by NICK LICATA not to discuss any LCN business with FRATIANNO" and "if he should again attempt to operate any racket activity and jeopardize any LCN business LICATA will issue a murder contract." (Bash Collection.)

Fearing for his life, Fratianno rekindled his relationship with the FBI in 1977. Coaxed by federal agent James Ahearn (right), he went from informant to government witness and began a countrywide tour of courtroom testimonies. (Niotta Collection.)

Posing in front of a pornography library during a bust amid Peter Milano's reign are two LAPD vice officers (above). The raid on bookies led by Chief Daryl Gates (right) came just prior. After Fratianno entered witness protection, mafia members began cooperating to avoid prison. Los Angeles soldier Craig Anthony "the Animal" Fiato and his brother Larry wore a wire for over a half dozen years, and in 1997, underboss Carmen Milano spilled information about members from Los Angeles, Las Vegas, and Cleveland. The feds formulated a five-page investigative report from Milano's intelligence, which also divulged the brugad's stigma. "The Los Angeles family is called the Mickey Mouse Mafia because they have very little control over the city," and "LCN family members from New Jersey and New York come into Los Angeles to make money and nothing is given to the Los Angeles family." (Both, Niotta Collection.)

Discover Thousands of Local History Books
Featuring Millions of Vintage Images

Arcadia Publishing, the leading local history publisher in the United States, is committed to making history accessible and meaningful through publishing books that celebrate and preserve the heritage of America's people and places.

Find more books like this at
www.arcadiapublishing.com

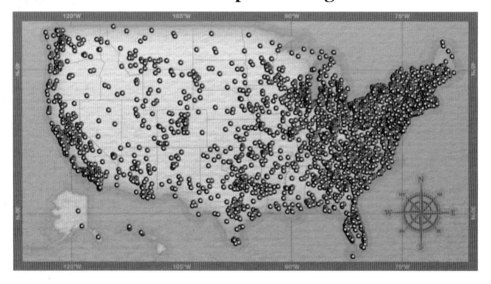

Search for your hometown history, your old stomping grounds, and even your favorite sports team.

Consistent with our mission to preserve history on a local level, this book was printed in South Carolina on American-made paper and manufactured entirely in the United States. Products carrying the accredited Forest Stewardship Council (FSC) label are printed on 100 percent FSC-certified paper.

MADE IN THE